DISASTER!

Revised edition; first published as *Canadian Disasters.*

René Schmidt

SCHOLASTIC CANADA LTD.

Scholastic Canada Ltd.
175 Hillmount Road, Markham, Ontario, Canada L6C 1Z7

Scholastic Inc.
555 Broadway, New York, NY 10012, USA

Scholastic Australia Pty Limited
PO Box 579, Gosford, NSW 2250, Australia

Scholastic New Zealand Limited
Private Bag 94407, Greenmount, Auckland, New Zealand

Scholastic Publications Ltd.
Villiers House, Clarendon Avenue, Leamington Spa,
Warwickshire CV32 5PR, UK

Edited by Laura Peetoom

Designed by Andrea Casault

Cover photograph: Arjen and Jerrine Verkaik/SKYART

Canadian Cataloguing in Publication Data
Schmidt, René
Disaster!

Rev. ed.
First ed. published under title: Canadian disasters.
Revised ed. 1999 has title: Disaster!
ISBN 0-439-98715-6

1. Disasters — Canada — Juvenile literature.
I. Title. II. Title: Canadian disasters.

FC176.S35 2000   j971   C00-930452-6
F1008.3.S35 2000

6 5 4 3 2   Printed in Canada   0 1 2 3 4/0

*I dedicate this book to my lovely wife Shirley,
who made sure I had the time to work on it and
helped edit my first drafts, and to my boys Adrian and
Daniel, who also helped find the boring parts.*

Acknowledgments

I would like to acknowledge those who helped me breathe a bit of life into their stories. For the Westray story, thanks to Shaun Comish, whose book and comments were invaluable, to Kenton Teasdale with his arresting recall of his son-in-law's last days, and to Larry Jahn, who shared details about his younger brother. I hope for success and some peace in your efforts for justice. My gratitude also goes to Ken Melanson, a retired Springhill miner who willingly shared details of his four days trapped in the Number Four Mine, and for his update on my story of the 1956 disaster.

Thanks to Jeff and Ruby Hoogsteen, whose inspiring faith after the ice storm turned their losses to gain, and Joshua and Denise Trimm for a child's perspective of the ice storm. Also to Mary Grandish, and Barbara and Debbie Molto, my thanks to you for describing a painful event. Thanks to Pat and Chris Koets, and Steven Dusa, who shared details of the clean-up effort in Winnipeg, and to all those who went and worked for the sake of other people. I am also grateful to old high school friends — Colonel Chris Shelley for technical information on air crashes, and Dr. Doug Sinclair for sharing memories of the Swissair crash.

Thanks to Kristen and Penny DeJong, who very early began to help with research on the internet, and also to my brother Erik for help in tracking things down. Thanks to my students Niki Dusa, Jodi Newton, Rebecca deWal, Charlotte Armstrong, Matthew Cameron, Rachel Kuracina and Robert Berry, who read the existing stories and gave me feedback on how they could be changed for the better.

Thanks to librarians Sharon Bugg and Robert Amesse, respectively of the Brighton and Quinte West Public Libraries, for their help in research.

And finally, thanks to Sandy Bogart Johnston and Laura Peetoom of Scholastic Canada for their patient work in editing the final manuscript.

Introduction

Disasters can occur anywhere, and to anybody. You could be involved in a disaster today or tomorrow. Sometimes they are caused by human beings, at others by the powerful and deadly forces of nature.

Accidental explosions can kill dozens of innocent people in seconds. A jet aircraft crashes and hundreds die in a few moments of screaming panic. One earthquake can destroy a mountain, change the route of a river or flatten a city. Storms can create waves high enough to twist and sink ships that try to run against them. Fires can scorch thousands of hectares of bush or forest, or they can burn whole towns, leaving the inhabitants homeless.

This book describes some of the disasters that have happened in Canada over the years. They are all true events. Some could have been prevented. Others were unavoidable. Many produced heroes: ordinary people in ordinary places who saved lives by doing extraordinary things when calamity struck.

As you read about these Canadian disasters, think about what you would have done if you had been there.

Table of Contents

5. Nature's Fury

6. Disaster on the Move

7. Recent Disasters

CHAPTER ONE

Canada's Worst Disaster

The Halifax Explosion

The worst disaster ever to happen in Canada occurred in 1917, in Halifax, Nova Scotia. It was the biggest accidental explosion in the history of the entire world — an explosion as big as that of a nuclear bomb. In a few terrible seconds, over 1600 people died and 6000 more were wounded.

It was World War I. German submarines were lurking underwater, waiting to torpedo English and Canadian vessels in the Atlantic Ocean. To guard against this, ships travelled in large groups called convoys, with navy warships to protect them. The convoys were formed in Halifax.

On the morning of December 6, an ammunition ship called the *Mont Blanc* was entering Halifax harbour. A freighter, the *Imo,* was heading out. The *Mont Blanc* was like a huge floating bomb: as long as a football field, twenty metres wide, and fully loaded with high explosives. For some reason, both ships steered for the same side of the narrow channel.

Big freighters are very hard to steer, and by the time the *Imo* began to change course it was too late. It ran into the *Mont Blanc,* ripping it open like a pop can. A fire started on board. For a few desperate minutes, the crew tried to put it out. Then they dropped everything and ran, knowing the ship was going to blow up and kill them all.

Only a few people on shore knew that the crippled vessel drifting in the harbour with blue flames licking from it was a loaded ammunition ship. One of them was a telegraph operator. He sent this message: "Ammunition ship on fire, drifting to Pier 9. Goodbye." His body was never found.

When the *Mont Blanc* exploded, a blizzard of metal, glass and wood fragments ripped through Halifax, mowing down everyone in its path. Many of the 6000 injured were blinded by the flying fragments. Pieces of the *Mont Blanc* fell all over the city and in the surrounding countryside. An anchor fell to earth five kilometres from the blast. A steel door landed four kilometres in the other direction. A sailor was hurled far into the air and landed on a hillside two kilometres away — unhurt, but wearing only his boots, his clothes torn off by the blast.

While a huge mushroom cloud formed in the sky, shock waves flattened almost all the buildings and homes of Halifax. Over a million square metres of Halifax were destroyed. A barn forty kilometres away was blown off its foundations. Ships far out at sea felt the jolt of the blast and feared they had been torpedoed. For a few moments the bottom of Halifax harbour could be seen, all the water momentarily blown out of it.

To make matters worse, soon after the explosion a freezing winter storm descended on the mutilated city and covered it with a blanket of snow. Many of the homeless had to endure hours of miserable cold

Shock waves flattened almost all the buildings in Halifax when the ammunition ship Mont Blanc exploded in Halifax harbour on December 6, 1917.

before they could find shelter.

Ships loaded with coffins, medical supplies and tents rushed to the port, while determined survivors started repairing the damage. Telephone and telegraph lines were reconnected. Power was restored and the injured were tended to.

Later, many of the victims of the explosion helped rebuild their city with pride. As a result of the disaster, Halifax became one of Canada's most modern cities, the first to be designed before being built.

CHAPTER TWO

Canada's Own *Titanic* Stories

The *Titanic* story has been told and retold. But many people are not aware of Canadian ships that rival the *Titanic's* bold history and tragic end. From the depths of the seas come these forgotten tales of arrogance, bravery and loss.

The Fourteen-Minute Disaster

The *Empress of Ireland* was a Canadian Pacific passenger liner built in 1906. After the *Titanic* sank in 1912, all passenger liners had to be equipped with enough lifeboats for all passengers, and their crews well trained in dealing with emergencies. Yet, on the night of May 29, 1914, on the St. Lawrence Seaway just past Rimouski, Quebec, all the training and all the life-saving equipment aboard couldn't prevent a terrible loss of life.

The *Storstad,* a Norwegian coal ship, fully laden and very heavy, was steaming upstream as the *Empress* headed downstream. A fog bank rolled in, and the captain of the *Empress* and the first mate of the *Storstad* each had to guess where the other ship was. Radar had not been invented yet.

Nobody can be sure just who was really at fault.

The mate of the *Storstad* was blamed for turning in the wrong direction in the fog; he claimed the *Empress* had turned in the wrong direction too. But Captain Kendall of the *Empress of Ireland* could only watch helplessly as the *Storstad* came looming out of the mist to ram his ship.

The waters of the St. Lawrence gushed into the enormous hole left by the *Storstad,* and the *Empress* quickly keeled over. The list, or tilt, on the ship prevented watertight doors from closing, so people in the lower-deck cabins were caught in their beds by the rushing water. Others woke in time to get out, only to be caught in the crowded hallways. Water poured into the boilers and the mighty engines died.

By now the ship was listing so badly that only the lifeboats on the side nearest the water could be lowered. In all the panic and confusion, sailors filled the boats with passengers and sent them out into the dark. Other passengers, life jackets on, jumped into the near-freezing water. On board were 170 Salvation Army officers. They gave their own life jackets to those who had none. Only twenty four of them were alive the next day.

Nearby, the *Storstad* was still floating, its bow crumpled by the accident, but its lifeboats in the water rescuing survivors from the *Empress.* Hundreds of cold, half-naked people were pulled from the water, too weak to move. Many others floated face down in the river, chilled to death. Other ships steamed to the rescue, but before they could arrive the *Empress of Ireland* rolled on her side and sank

The Empress of Ireland before the fatal collision.

from view. Only fourteen minutes had passed since she was hit.

The hero of the night was Doctor James Grant. Half-frozen and half-naked himself, no sooner was he pulled from the water and taken aboard the *Storstad* than he began reviving people and instructing others, as well as setting bones and comforting those beyond medical help. When a near-riot broke out between a group of people who all spoke different languages, he stopped the trouble unaided. While he was attending the chief engineer of the *Empress*, a half-crazed man barged in and threatened the doctor. James Grant knocked the man out and continued with his work.

The river claimed 1012 people that night, 840 of whom were passengers. Most of their bodies were never recovered. The wreck of the *Empress of Ireland* still lies at the bottom of the St. Lawrence in fifty metres of water. Even as you read this, ships are passing above her remains, the final resting place for hundreds of the victims of Canada's worst marine disaster.

November 1913:
The Forgotten Killer

Ocean-going sailors like to make fun of Great Lakes sailors. They believe that only the high seas can produce the kind of danger that shapes a true sailor. But they are wrong. There have been more than 8000 shipwrecks on the Great Lakes in the last few hundred years; every year in the late fall the Great Lakes produce some of nature's deadliest storms.

The November storms are the worst. But most ships' captains try to push their freighters through, since each completed trip earns thousands of dollars of revenue. The storms come and the ships survive, year in, year out. If a storm is too severe, a ship can always take shelter in the lee of an island or a point and let the land block the wind. Sometimes a storm is so bad a ship is driven ashore, dragging its anchors behind it.

In the spring of 1913, the *James Carruthers,* then Canada's newest ship, slid into the calm waters beside the Collingwood, Ontario shipyards. The water roared aside for her and then came back to surround her again as she bobbed and rolled before settling down to an even keel. She was the largest freight ship in the British Commonwealth, 170 elegant metres of lean, proud steel, and she was Canadian. Set down in a city, she would have extended one and a half blocks. Her modern steam engine was powerful, and only one or two American ships could carry as much cargo as the *James Carruthers.*

Still, people did not brag too much about her. Just a year before, the *Titanic* had sunk on her maiden voyage, leaving people more careful about calling their largest ships "unsinkable."

Half a year and three journeys later, on November 7, the *James Carruthers* was heading north out of the St. Clair River into Lake Huron. In ports around Lakes Huron, Ontario, Superior and Michigan, the red flags were up to warn ships of a severe storm. Many captains, Captain Wright of the *James Carruthers* among them, ignored the warnings. Weather forecasting was a new science and often wrong, and the weather so far this November had been mild.

The winds did not die out as most believed they would, but grew stronger every hour. The temperature dropped, and ice formed quickly on steel decks and cabins, an unwanted cargo weighing many more tonnes than the ships were made to bear safely. Each breaking wave added a new ice layer. Crews watched helplessly, unable to chop it away, for anyone stepping out onto the deck in such high winds would have been swept away to certain death in the freezing lake.

Captains reported that at the height of the storm the waves came in groups of three and the wind changed direction frequently. Sometimes it blew crosswise to the waves, making steering the ice-encrusted ships almost impossible. The storm was at its most intense for twelve long hours throughout Friday night. Even after that, the shrieking wind,

The James Carruthers less than six months before the storms of November, 1913 sank her along with twenty-two crew members.

blowing sometimes at a hundred kilometres an hour, continued through the whole of Saturday and Sunday. Waves were whipped up nine to twelve metres high. Captains tried to avoid being rolled over by these monsters by running with them. But these were not like the long ocean swells, which lift ships like bits of wood and drop them down again. These waves were shorter and steeper than ocean waves, capable of lifting each end of a freighter and leaving the middle unsupported. Even modern ships are not built to take that kind of stress for long.

The *James Carruthers* struggled to survive the terrible pounding, and lasted until late Saturday night, then went to the bottom somewhere north of Goderich, Ontario, taking twenty-two crew members with her.

Farther from shore, unseen by anyone, some of the worlds' finest ships met their ends. Large American lake freighters the *Isaac M. Scott* and the *Charles S. Price* broke up, throwing their shouting sailors into the freezing waters. American sister ships the *Argus* and the *Hydrus,* carrying twenty-four men each, sank unwitnessed, somewhere on Lake Huron. The Canadian ship *Wexford,* built years before in the finest British shipyards, sank with all hands. It had survived the worst weather on the oceans of the world, but succumbed to this Lake Huron storm. Early on Monday morning, her horn was heard blowing a distress signal for hours, a cry for help which could not be answered by anyone on shore. And many ships and their doomed crews became, simply, unknown wrecks in an unconcerned lake.

Finally the wind and waves died down and bodies began floating ashore along the Ontario coastline of Lake Huron. And people began to wonder — what exactly had happened during those long, drawn-out hours? Crew members from an American ship were washed ashore in life jackets from the *Wexford*. A stewardess from the *Argus* floated ashore wearing the engineer's greatcoat and the captain's life jacket. What tales of rescue, courage and self-sacrifice are left untold?

Two hundred and forty-four sailors died and thirty-eight ships were stranded or completely destroyed in that single three-day storm. There has never been another that has done so much damage to so many large steel-hulled ships on inland waterways. When the *Edmund Fitzgerald* sank in 1975, the world was amazed that such a large freighter could go down with all hands. The 1913 storm sank eight such ships, some of which were almost the same size as the *Fitzgerald*.

For weeks after the storm, families travelled to shoreline towns to try to find the bodies of loved ones. Some were never identified. A memorial headstone in a Goderich graveyard stands above the spot where five unidentified seamen lie buried. The single word proudly and simply tells what these people were: SAILORS.

The Wreck of the
Edmund Fitzgerald

When she was launched in 1958, the *Edmund Fitzgerald* was the largest ship on the Great Lakes, and the largest ship ever to sail on fresh water: just a little shorter than the *Titanic,* and carrying just a bit less weight, fully loaded. *"Big Fitz"* was as long as two city blocks. Stood on end, she would have been as tall as a seventy-two-storey skyscraper.

Over the years she had sailed the big lakes end to end, hundreds of trips, carrying iron ore from the dusty railroad docks on the western tip of Lake Superior to the smoky steel mills on Lake Erie and Lake Michigan. In time, other monster ships were built which were the same size or slightly larger. But to the older sailors on the Great Lakes, the *Edmund Fitzgerald* was still a special ship, a champion of size and power. By November of 1975, she had sailed over a million and a half kilometres on the Great Lakes.

The *Fitzgerald* had one of the best crews of any ship. Some of the men on her were new to the life of a large ship, but most had long experience. Captain Ernest McSorley was respected by all who knew him. Jack McCarthy was a captain in his own right, but signed aboard the *Fitzgerald* as First Mate to join his old friend McSorley. Most of the crew had many long years of experience on the Great Lakes, and many had also sailed on the oceans.

The Great Lakes hadn't changed since the loss of

On November 9, 1975, "Big Fitz" went down with all hands. Twenty-nine sailors drowned.

the *James Carruthers* in 1913. November still meant sudden, vicious storms. But the use of satellites and weather stations to predict and monitor storms, and radar to guide ships through them, had made our Great Lakes less deadly. Gale force winds were known about beforehand, and wise sailors knew what to do. Smaller craft found shelter in harbours, and did not venture out for any reason. Mid-size yachts and working vessels tied up too, or steered courses to the lee side of land, to let it block the raging wind and waves when they came.

On November 9, 1975, a storm was predicted for the Great Lakes region. And it would be big. Out on Lake Superior, only large freighters like the *Edmund Fitzgerald* and the newer *Arthur Anderson* dared venture out of sight of shore, and even they prepared for trouble. Officers checked and rechecked all the cargo hatches while the crew tightened every clamp. Anything loose on deck was removed or secured, and a heightened sense of alertness came over all the men. As the wind picked up speed, sailors going from the front to the rear of the ships stayed off the open deck. Instead they walked the gloomy steel passageways below decks, avoiding the biting cold and the risk of being washed overboard by an uncaring wave. The storm was large and circular and of unusual force. It was almost a hurricane, and its furious centre was moving directly over Lake Superior, sweeping down on the ships. Captain Bernie Cooper on the *Anderson* kept in touch with the *Fitzgerald* over the radio. Both captains agreed that they might be able to avoid the worst of the storm by heading for the northern, Canadian coast of Lake Superior. So they changed course.

By now the wind was a steady 90 kilometres an hour and gusting up to 140 kilometres, tearing the tops off waves and hurling them onto ships and shore and men. The waves rammed the ships' sides, sharp and punishing. They lifted each end of the *Arthur Anderson,* and the poor ship groaned and shrieked as wind and waves twisted her unmercifully.

Yet, the two ships pressed on. Gradually the *Fitzgerald,* the faster of the two lake freighters, pulled ahead of the *Anderson.*

At about 1 P.M. on November 9, both ships passed through the eye of the storm. A warm sun and calm water greeted them, and for a brief two hours, things were calm. Then the storm returned and the winds came from the other direction.

From the bridge of the *Anderson,* Captain Cooper saw the *Fitzgerald* pass close to a dangerous site called Six Fathom Shoal. Many sailors knew that the shoal was not marked properly on their maps. Dangerous rocks lay unseen a kilometre and a half farther north than the charts indicated. Cooper told his mate not to go as close as the *Fitzgerald* had done. A few minutes later, McSorley radioed him with some troubling news: he had water coming in and waves had knocked away two vents and done some damage on his deck. Both his ballast pumps were going and the ship was listing. Would the *Anderson* stay close to the *Fitzgerald* across the lake?

Cooper agreed. But he could not help but wonder: Had the *Edmund Fitzgerald* hit bottom on Six Fathom Shoal and ripped an opening in her hull? McSorley hadn't said anything about it, but Cooper thought he heard fear in the other captain's voice. Later, at an inquest, there would be many questions about the next few hours.

The rain had begun again and with the high winds there was no hope of seeing clearly. In the pilot house of each ship, officers only had their radar to watch out for other ships and the shoreline. At 6:30 a deadly combination of two enormous waves put the *Arthur Anderson*'s main deck under four metres of water. For a few terrifying seconds, only the wheelhouse and aft cabins were above water. Then the large ore carrier came back up, shaking off the water like a dog.

Somewhere, a few kilometres away, the *Fitzgerald* took the same waves. How had the ship reacted? How much water was in her holds now? Captain McSorley radioed the *Anderson* that he had lost his radar. Could the *Anderson* guide him the rest of the way to Whitefish Bay? *"The Fitz"* could not find her way in the storm alone.

On board both ships, nervous off-duty crews huddled in crews' quarters and talked away their fears. The ones who were working fought against the dread and panic which such terrible storms cause. Some said prayers or wrote letters, wondering if either would be answered. The chief engineer of the

Fitzgerald, George Holl, had once been asked by a young crewman if lifeboats could be launched in heavy seas if the ship broke up. His reply was realistic: "As far as I'm concerned, I'd just crawl in my bunk and pull the blankets over my head."

At 7:10, the *Anderson*'s first mate radioed that a ship was passing to the west of the *Fitzgerald*. He asked how the *Fitzgerald* was making out with her problems.

"We are holding our own," said McSorley — the last words to be heard from the *Edmund Fitzgerald*.

Experts would later suggest that ahead of the *Anderson,* in the darkness of the storm, the *Fitzgerald* was riding lower and lower in the stormy lake water. Then, too suddenly for the ship to send a warning, her end came. A wave crashed over her bow and forced it downward into the lake. The water in her holds roared forward, forcing her bow down farther, into a fatal plunge. The heavy cargo of iron ore came next, crashing forward through heavy steel cargo walls and spilling out of her forward deck hatches, twisting the heavy steel plate as if it were thin sheet metal. In the rear of the ship, pockets of air roared upward and outward, bursting windows and woodwork with a hurricane force before escaping outward into the night. Water stormed in through all openings and burst metal seams. The ship broke in half, spilling its cargo into the midnight dark waters of Lake Superior. The crew of twenty-nine men never had a chance. Most were likely killed in an instant. Their bodies, trapped in the wreckage, joined the ship's steel carcass in 160 metres of cold water.

For a while, the crew of the *Anderson* was busy with the task of fighting the deadly waves while struggling to get to Whitefish Bay and calmer waters. They were unaware that they were sailing over the place where, minutes before, the *Fitzgerald* had gone to her final rest. When one of the crew checked his radar, the *Fitzgerald* was gone. Frantic searching and calling other ships on the phone revealed nothing. There was no large, red-painted bulk carrier. She had disappeared.

The Coast Guard was notified that the ship was missing. Unfortunately, their vessel *Naugatuk* was unable to search the stormy waters off Whitefish Point because it was too small for such a storm.

The call went out to all the ships at anchor in Whitefish Bay. The law of the sea is that sailors help each other, regardless of nationality. But a captain is also directly responsible for the safety of his ship and his crew. Several ocean-going ships decided it was too risky, and stayed at anchor. The Coast Guard called Captain Cooper. Would the *Anderson* go out again into the storm and look for survivors of the *Edmund Fitzgerald?* The decision was a terrible one to make, yet Cooper agreed to go. So did another ore carrier, the *William Clay Ford.*

They found a smashed-in *Fitzgerald* lifeboat thirteen kilometres from the site of the sinking, plus a few life jackets and other debris floating sadly on the surface. The next day another lifeboat was found.

There were no survivors, and not a single body was recovered.

In Detroit, Father Ingalls of the Old Mariners' Church received an early morning call from an old friend. He went to his little church, the scene of many such sad messages in the past. Father Ingalls climbed the old bell tower and began to ring the steeple bell. He didn't know the men he was ringing for, not even their names, but twenty-nine times he swung that bell, once for each of the poor souls aboard the *Edmund Fitzgerald*.

Respect the Sea

Since the first explorers dared to sail out of sight of land, going out to sea has held a special danger. Canada is a maritime nation, and the people on our coastlines have learned to respect the sea and all its fury. Many families have stories of shipwreck and survival in their histories. But sometimes people forget the hard-learned lessons. Carelessness, overconfidence and a lack of good judgement characterize these three tragic stories.

Death on the Ice

In Newfoundland in the early 1900s, fishermen relied on the seal hunt for their winter livelihood. The two dollars they received for each pelt made it possible to endure the unpleasant work and terrible conditions, and men scrambled to secure places on sealing ships. Many of the ships' captains cared nothing for the sealers. All they were interested in was loading up with as many pelts as they could carry. The hunters had to make their own hot food on the open deck and find a place to sleep wherever they could.

In 1914 an old wooden ship, the *Newfoundland,* set off with a full load of fishermen for the seal hunt, but the underpowered vessel got stuck in the ice. Captain Wes Keane knew that the *Stephano,* commanded by his father, was ahead. After being stuck three days, he suggested that the men walk across the ice to the location of the hunt. If the weather deteriorated they could take shelter on his father's ship.

The Bonaventure, Florizel, Stephano and Newfoundland. All four ships were involved in the seal hunt disaster.

After a long, cold walk, the men came upon old Captain Abram Keane and the *Stephano*. He took them aboard and sailed to the site of the hunt, where he dropped them off. Before leaving them, he told the sealers not to return to his vessel, but to walk back to their own ship when they were done. Nobody dared question the powerful old captain, and when the time came, they set out on the long walk back to the *Newfoundland*.

About halfway back, a blinding storm swooped down on them and within moments all the landmarks looked the same. The *Newfoundland* had no radio aboard, and Wes Keane, not knowing that the men were supposed to be returning to his ship, believed the hunters to be safely aboard the *Stephano*. His father assumed they were back aboard the *Newfoundland*. Nobody had any idea that the men were missing, lost on the ice.

For two days the hunters struggled to survive. One of them, Jessie Collins, bravely pushed, slapped and cheered the men on, keeping them moving — keeping them alive. But despite his untiring efforts, many men simply froze to death where they stood, or while praying, or when they fell asleep. A father was found standing with his sons, their arms around each other, frozen to the spot. One young man, Cecil Mouland, kept himself alive by sheer stubbornness, determined that no other man would marry his fiancée.

Finally, Captain Wes Keane spotted the frozen band on the ice. Out of the 123 men who had set out, only 46 were still alive.

The blame for the tragedy was laid on the shoulders of Captain Abram Keane for failing to make sure the men were safe. As a result of the experience, all sealing ships were advised to carry radios in the future.

Death of a Princess

About four years later, on the morning of October 24, 1918, a Canadian passenger ship, the *Princess Sophia,* was caught in a blizzard and driven off course near the coast of Alaska. Running at full speed, the ship crashed onto the rocks of Vanderbilt Reef and lodged there. Captain Locke was confident that although his vessel was stuck right then, the next high tide would lift it clear. There were no holes in the hull. Details of the situation were radioed to the owners of the ship, Canadian Pacific Railway in Victoria, assuring them that everyone on board was safe.

The CPR decided to take no chances and sent another ship, the *Princess Alice,* to bring the passengers back, as well as a salvage ship to help the *Princess Sophia.* American ships also heard the radio exchanges and they too steamed to the aid of the *Princess Sophia.* They hove to, ready to take those aboard to the nearby shore. But Captain Locke decided there was no need to disturb the passengers by sending them out into the cold, snowy night. The sea was flat and calm and they were warm and safe on board the ship.

But then, with no warning, the falling snow turned into a wicked storm. The wind rose to a howl. Huge waves, metres high, sprang out of the flat sea to pummel the small American rescue ships anchored around the *Sophia*. They retreated quickly to the shelter of a small island nearby. Now the wind began to move the *Princess Sophia* as well. A particularly strong gust pushed the stern of the ship around, and the bottom of the hull tore on the rocks like tinfoil. The shift also dislodged the ship. She drifted free and immediately began to sink. The radio operator signalled, "Just in time to say goodbye. We are foundering." In the howling storm the small American ships were unable to get through to the dying vessel, so close by. The other CPR ships were still a long way off.

The Princess Sophia *at sea.*

By the next morning, only the short mast at the bow of the *Princess Sophia* could be seen above the water. Bodies floated everywhere. It was the sad duty of the captain of the *Princess Alice* to report that not one person from the ship had survived the night. All 343 men, women and children were dead.

One sea captain later claimed that the water was so calm before the storm that the passengers could have been safely taken ashore by canoe. The sinking of this proud Canadian Pacific ship remains the worst disaster at sea on our west coast.

Death in the Cold Atlantic

The people of Newfoundland are surrounded by the sea, and they have learned over centuries to respect it. Why was it, then, that one of Canada's most preventable disasters happened so close to its rocky shores? The tragedy happened in 1982, and the terrible waste of life made headlines around the world.

An enormous floating drilling rig called the Ocean Ranger was stationed like a small city off the coast of Newfoundland. It was anchored in the Atlantic while the workers aboard drilled into the sea bed searching for oil trapped beneath the Grand Banks. About half of the eighty-four men and women aboard were Canadians, mostly from Newfoundland; the other half, Americans. The rig itself was owned by an American company.

The most senior person on the rig wasn't a sea captain, or any kind of sailor at all. He was a Tool Pusher, an expert drilling-rig engineer whose knowledge lay in drilling, not in seamanship. In the urgent business of drilling for oil not enough thought was given to safety, or the possible hazards of being at sea. There were life jackets, but of the wrong type. There were no "survival suits," designed to preserve life in freezing water. There were lifeboats, but they were of two different kinds, and nobody was sure if all the workers knew how to use them. In fact, some of the lifeboats hadn't even been installed when disaster struck in 1982.

There were basic problems with the design of the Ocean Ranger right from the start. The sea-going heart of a drilling rig is the ballast control room. This is the control centre which keeps the vessel floating evenly and steadily. It should have been placed high up, as a bridge is placed on a ship, where ice and waves have the least chance of doing any damage. But instead, it was positioned halfway up one of the giant legs. This kept it above the calm water, but not above the waves of a severe storm.

On Valentine's Day, 1982, the rig was shaken by the howling winds of a freezing winter storm. Huge waves smashed against the floating platform, causing it to shudder and strain against the twelve anchors holding it in place. Then one particularly big wave came crashing through the window of the ballast control room.

Immediately, the salt water short-circuited the rig's electrical system. The operator on duty could still use hand controls — but this operator didn't know how. It was time to let others know about the emergency. But the intercom system that connected the ballast control room to the rest of the rig was useless; at some point it had broken down and never been repaired.

At 1:05 A.M. on Sunday, February 15, the foreman of the Ocean Ranger radioed that the rig had a tilt to the left that couldn't be corrected — what sailors call a port list. This would be bad enough in calm water. In a storm it was disastrous.

The supply ship for the Ocean Ranger, the *Seaforth Highlander,* was immediately sent to the rescue, along with the supply ships serving two other

drilling rigs. At 1:30 A.M. the Ocean Ranger reported that the workers had been ordered to take to the
lifeboats. One by one the boats were launched into
the towering seas by the inexperienced workers, and
one by one they crashed into the enormous pillars of
the rig and sank, or were flipped over by the first
wave they encountered.

Now the lack of survival suits became a life-and-

*Eighty-four crew members died in the frigid Atlantic waters off
Newfoundland when the rig collapsed in February, 1982.
(CP LASERPHOTO)*

death problem. Every second counted as the supply ships struggled through the freezing Atlantic toward the eighty-four men and women of the Ocean Ranger. By the time the *Seaforth Highlander* got to the scene, less than an hour after being dispatched, only one lifeboat was afloat with living people inside, and it was badly damaged. The ship manoeuvred alongside. The quaking passengers were almost within arm's reach of rescue when the lifeboat slowly rolled over, throwing its occupants, some wearing only pyjamas, into the sea. Before the *Seaforth Highlander* could come around again through the waves, the unlucky passengers were all dead.

For hours the three supply ships criss-crossed the area. By about 3:00 A.M. the Ocean Ranger itself had sunk completely from sight, leaving the sea littered with wreckage and floating bodies. Not one person aboard the drilling rig survived.

An investigation by the Canadian and Newfoundland governments decided that the disaster was directly linked to equipment failures and poor training. Every drilling rig is now under the overall command of a sea captain who has the last word on safety. Practice emergency drills are held regularly, and workers can be fired if they fail to attend. The loss of eighty-four lives and a multi-million dollar drilling rig taught the oil industry what sailors around the world have always known: The sea must be respected.

CHAPTER THREE

Fire!

Just like the sea, fire is a mighty enemy that humankind has learned to use as a tool. But from time to time, the tool rises up and strikes back, its awesome power directed against its would-be master. . . .

Canada's Worst Fire

Fire these days, although dangerous and fearsome, isn't quite the problem it used to be. Now firefighters have trucks with pumps and hoses, and even convenient hydrants to connect them to. But for early Canadians fire was always something to be dreaded: it became uncontrollable so quickly. If you lived in the country, in the winter, a fire could mean death in two ways: you might escape your burning house alive, but freeze to death before you could reach your nearest neighbour. In the cities, a fire could demolish whole blocks of wooden houses before the flames finally burned themselves out.

But there is one type of fire where things have not changed. If a forest fire approaches today you do the same as you would have done fifty or a hundred years ago. You run for your life.

Canada's worst fire was a forest fire that overran the entire town of Matheson, Ontario, in 1916. William Dowson was only nineteen when he lived through the Matheson fire. He was sitting in a small shack, talking with friends. They knew a forest fire was burning a few kilometres away from them. Suddenly, a blast of hot wind swept down and shook the shack — like a "giant hand" — and surrounded it with thick smoke.

The men got out, expecting the shack to burst into flames, understanding immediately what great danger they were in. Dowson went to his tent to get ready to leave. The main body of the fire was still about sixteen kilometres away, but he could feel the heat in his face, and even through his clothes. And he could hear it, "a continuous roaring sound like a freight train; ominous and deep sounding."

Dowson, his friends and some others were picked up by train and carried away from the fire's front. The fire came roaring after them, its intense heat leaving the tracks twisted and useless. William didn't go far on the train, though, deciding to stay in town to try to save what he could. Soon he found himself surrounded by fire on every side:

"For hours I had moved fast in temperatures that could have reached about 130 degrees and much more. . . . My legs let go. A voice reached me: 'Get up.' "

It was still afternoon, yet it was as dark as night. Dowson's fatigue, the heat and the choking smoke made it difficult to breathe. As well, the uprush of heat carried a lot of breathable air with it, hundreds of metres into the sky, leaving a vacuum that wind rushed in to fill.

Ahead of him, Dowson saw an opening. A curtain of flame swept in, and he hesitated. The comparative cool on the other side coaxed him forward again. He faced the fire and dashed forward, eyes closed, through a mass of red-orange flame. "The great fire wrapped about me for a moment — a solid mass of combustion like the interior of a furnace. Then I was through and in a clearing. . . . "

William Dowson collapsed in the clearing, but he was on ground high enough that he got oxygen, so he survived. Many others were not as lucky. Wading into creeks and rivers, they suffocated when the oxygen around them was used up by the fire. Others stayed too long to try to save their homes and were caught in the roaring flames. Later, William regained consciousness and explored the ravaged town:

"We lost all track of time. We just enjoyed the air, which seemed so clear and cool. All around us the great land glowed from the golden glow of the afterburning. Nothing remained but the fairly thick stubs of trees. Some of these burned like candles. In others, irregularly set pockets of fire glowed and sparkled. Occasionally a pocket near the base of one would burn almost through. Slowly it would bend toward the glowing earth, then, as its burning fibres gave way, fall quickly, to land with a soft thud, sending out from its sides clouds of soft ashes. . . . "

A few bewildered men wandered aimlessly. No one knew what to do. The railway was silenced. On a siding, a still-burning fire consumed a coal car. Its

A girl and her grandfather stand amid the burnt-out remains of their home following the Matheson fire. (William Dowson)

steel wheels slowly melted down to slump like mud around the steel rails of the track. North of the tracks, where most of Matheson had been situated, nothing was left. The tracks south of the town were ruined, and their bridges probably destroyed. There was death and desolation under a bright clear sky and soft summer breeze, less than twenty-four hours after the fiery disaster had roared through.

The Matheson fire was Canada's worst killer fire. Two hundred people died in the heat and flames. William Dowson took some of the only photos of the destruction; without them, the impact of the disaster might have been lost.

The government supplied lumber and building materials for the replacement of destroyed homes. The survivors provided their own labour. For the elderly this was impossible, so the government also built some small places for the elderly at their home sites. After that, with no pensions and no welfare, they were on their own.

And so, the residents of Matheson rebuilt their town. It still exists, near Timmins, Ontario — surrounded by hundreds of kilometres of new-grown forest.

City Fires

The Vancouver Fire

Vancouver is one of Canada's most beautiful cities and a world-class seaport and industrial centre. Like many Canadian cities, it suffered a major fire in its early years.

The fur traders and gold miners were the first to come to the B.C. coast, and when they moved on, the lumber mills moved in. Sawmills appeared on nearly every river, and towns like Port Moody and New Westminster looked as if they would attract all the new settlers. But then the small town of Granville, nicknamed Gastown, became the last stop for the newly built Canadian Pacific Railway. A new town, Vancouver, began to grow like a wild thing, spreading out onto nearby hillsides and the tree-lined mountain slopes. Forests were stripped of their timber, and leftover branches and stumps, called slash, lay drying in heaps at the edge of every road and clearing.

The hot June sun in 1886 dried the slash completely and baked the ground a hard, dusty brown. On June 13, a fire began somewhere in the woods to the north of Vancouver. It raced into town, and people began to run. Some stayed just long enough to put on their shoes — and were trapped by the flames. In one part of town people huddled in a ditch, watching while others just a few metres away burned to death. Some hid in wells, only to be suffocated when the oxygen in the air was consumed

A typical Vancouver street scene, before the fire.

by the fire raging above them.

Most ran for the safety of the cool salt water of Burrard Inlet. There they hastily built rafts and pushed them out into the water. It was too danger- ous to stay on the shore. According to one witness, the houses would "blister on the bare boards and shimmer a moment or two with the heat waves. Then the whole outside of the building would be a mass of white flame."

After a few hours, the fire burned itself out. The amazing thing is the speed with which the city was

Vancouver policemen outside the makeshift city hall one day after the fire.

rebuilt. Tents were erected to replace stores and the smouldering city hall. Cities that usually competed with Vancouver helped out. New Westminster sent lumber that very day, along with $9000 in cash — a lot of money in those days. Within twelve hours, the actual rebuilding had begun, and before long, Vancouver was bigger than it had been before.

The Toronto Fire

Toronto also experienced a great fire during a time of strong growth, in the early 1900s. More and more immigrants were coming from Europe to settle in the New World. Toronto's plain wooden buildings were quickly replaced by impressive structures. By 1904, Toronto had its own "Flatiron" building, to rival the one in New York. It occupied a triangle-shaped lot in the heart of town, and reminded people of the irons used at the time to press clothing. It was an impressive five storeys high! Timothy Eaton's new store had real escalators — which entertained Toronto children for hours on end. The large stone City Hall was also impressive, and the steeple on St. James cathedral was the tallest in North America.

Unfortunately, Toronto's growth was so fast that safety standards had not kept up. The truth of this came to light — firelight — on the night of April 19, 1904. A fire began at the E&S Currie building at 60 Wellington St., in the heart of the business district. A night watchman reported the fire and firemen were quickly on the scene, but insufficient water pressure and outdated equipment spoiled their

Ninety-eight buildings were destroyed in the 1904 fire that devastated Toronto's downtown business district.

efforts. Strong winds fanned the flames, spreading the blaze to other buildings nearby, buildings with stone fronts but wooden insides. One after another, they were quickly consumed by the blaze.

A vast section of the city's core, including 98 buildings containing 137 businesses, was completely destroyed by the fire. A smouldering ruin was all that was left of one of the busiest downtown areas of the city. Yet, unlike major fires in many cities — and luckily for Toronto — nobody was killed in the great fire of 1904.

The Saddest Fire

It was a bright but cold Sunday on January 9, 1927. More than 1000 Montreal children lined up at the Laurier Palace Theatre on St. Catherine Street to see the afternoon movies. Although the law in those days said that children had to bring someone over the age of sixteen with them, many didn't, and managed to get in anyway. The program usually consisted of a newsreel, several cartoons and two movies. It was a popular way to spend a Sunday afternoon.

Kids had to pay a precious quarter for seats in the main part of the theatre, while seats in the balcony cost only fifteen cents. Often there were just not enough of these cheaper seats available to accommodate all the kids who wanted them, and many ended up standing in the aisles instead.

On this particular Sunday, the movies were *Sparrows,* with Mary Pickford, and a comedy called *Get 'Em Young.* The kids were enjoying the comedy when suddenly a boy spotted a curl of smoke at his feet. *"Le feu! Le feu!"* he shouted. Immediately kids all around stood up to see.

Down below, on the main floor of the theatre, the children saw the flames and rushed for the exits. Smoke began to billow out along the ceiling, adding to the compulsion to get out into the clean winter air. Up in the balcony, the few adults tried to prevent panic, but they couldn't stop a rush for the exits on both sides of the balcony. Then, at the stairs leading from the balcony's eastern exit, a tragedy began to unfold.

Just five short steps from the sidewalk, some of the smaller children tripped on the stairs and fell. Those behind crashed on top of them. Behind them, kids coming down the steps pushed to get out. In no time the whole stairway was filled from top to bottom with a mass of fallen children, all struggling to get free.

Firefighters were quickly on the scene, but it was impossible to pull individuals free from the tangled heap, or even to get past the two sharp bends in the stairway. Soon smoke was pouring down over the children, adding to the chaos. Water was sprayed over the crush of bodies while holes were desperately chopped in the walls beside the stairway and underneath it.

Constable Albert Boisseau was off duty, but he happened to be near the theatre and was one of the first rescuers on the scene. Among the dead children he eventually carried out of the theatre was his eldest daughter, who was supposed to have been skating with friends. Later he learned that his other two children had also died, suffocated on the stairway. Another family, the Quintals of Joliette Street, also lost three children in the disaster.

One of the firefighters, Alphage Arpin, was sick with fear when he arrived at the theatre. He knew his own son had gone there that day. He was unable to find him among either the living or the dead at the theatre, but was heartbroken when he later found him at the morgue where dozens of the victims had been taken.

One boy, Roger Frappier, could well have been among the dead had it not been for his quick thinking. He was close to the fire when it started and he soon saw that he would never be able to escape through the eastern exit. Instead, he jumped from the balcony to one of the aisles below. Although he was injured in the fall, he did escape with his life.

Altogether, seventy-seven people died in the fire. Most of them were children between the ages of eight and twelve. All of them died on the eastern stairway. Since that disaster, theatres have had to obey strict laws dealing with the supervision of children, and people are no longer allowed to stand in the aisles.

Moving Death-Traps

The Dugald Train Wreck

It was the end of the summer holidays for many Winnipeggers who had been vacationing in the cottage country of Lake of the Woods. They were travelling home on an old wooden passenger train which had started out from Minaki, Ontario, returning people to jobs and schools in Winnipeg and nearby towns.

The train should have been taken out of service years earlier, but it had been kept running because of World War II. Now the war was over, but such trains had still not been retired, despite the fact that they were very dangerous. Made out of wood, they weren't nearly as strong as the new steel coaches. Besides, they were a fire hazard: instead of electricity, the cars were lit with gas, which was carried in large tanks beneath the coaches.

At 10:50 P.M. on September 1, 1947, the Minaki train rolled toward a CNR transcontinental train stopped at Dugald, about thirty kilometres east of Winnipeg. What the engineer didn't know was that both trains were on the same track. The Minaki train slammed into the transcontinental, and several of the old wooden cars smashed to pieces and derailed.

Gerald Shields was working not far away when

the accident happened. He ran to the wreck and was able to pull five dazed passengers from the splintered cars before fire broke out and the searing flames drove him and other rescuers back.

Many people were still trapped inside the train, calling for help, but the fires were fed by broken gas lines and the big gas tanks themselves. There was no hope for those who weren't immediately pulled free. Most of the more than forty dead were in the first two passenger cars of the Minaki train. The transcontinental, a modern train with steel coaches, was not derailed by the crash, and its passengers were only shaken up.

The *Noronic* Fire

Two years later, a needless fire destroyed a $3.5 million ship and took the lives of 118 of its passengers. The ship was the *Noronic,* owned by Canada Steamship Lines. It could carry almost 600 passengers. Over 100 metres long, it had five decks and several fine restaurants and bars. In those days passenger ships like the *Noronic* were very popular as tour boats on all the Great Lakes.

But the *Noronic* was a death trap. Today such a ship would never be allowed to carry passengers, and sailors would refuse to sign aboard it. The hull and decks were made of steel, but everything else was made of wood. Yet there was no sprinkler system and many of the fire hoses didn't work. Worse still — and even though the *Noronic*'s sister ship, the *Hamonic,* had been destroyed in a blaze just four years

The bow of the burning Noronic *as firefighters hose her with water. (Gilbert A. Milne)*

earlier — the sailors on the *Noronic* weren't properly instructed in fire control.

On September 17, 1949, the ship tied up at Pier 9 in Toronto. About 1:15 in the morning, a small fire broke out in a closet where maids sometimes hid to smoke cigarettes. A passenger and a porter found the fire and ran for the nearest firehose, but it didn't work.

By the time an alarm was sent to the Toronto

fire department, the blaze was already out of control. The fire had raced along a passenger hallway and smoke was rapidly filling the ship. Sleepy passengers, frightened by the smoke, panicked and ran in all directions. The dry, painted wood burned like kindling.

On the bow of the *Noronic,* some women tried to climb down ladders onto the dock. A few men started to push them aside so they could go down first. Two brothers, Art and Gordon Alves, pitched the men into the black water and let the women go ahead. Also in the bow, two little sisters waited calmly while many adults around them panicked. Art Alves found six-year-old Barbara Kerr waiting and told her to ride piggyback while he climbed down a rope. Barbara's eight-year-old sister climbed down a glowing-hot steel cable. She burned her hands, but saved her own life — one of 500 passengers who survived the fire.

Dozens of people jumped into the water and drowned trying to escape the flaming death on the ship, as the foghorn blew with an insane shrieking all through the night. A total of 118 people are known to have died in the fire, though only 104 bodies were ever recovered. The ship itself was a total loss.

Soon after the *Noronic* tragedy, laws were made to ensure that all passenger ships had sprinkler systems and firefighting equipment that worked properly. Nobody wanted to be responsible for another fire like the one that destroyed the *Noronic.*

Of the ship, only the foghorn remains, dulled and aged by the heat of the fire. It sits on display in the Marine Museum of Toronto. When it blows its low, sad note, you can almost feel the flames and panic of September 17, 1949.

When the Earth Breaks

The following stories are dedicated especially to miners. Mining is one of civilization's oldest jobs. For centuries, miners have used sweat and muscle to dig riches out of the vast storehouses of the earth. These days, explosives and machinery have replaced the pickaxe and shovel, but mining is still a difficult and dangerous job. Canadian miners have been involved in some of the most unforgettable disasters of the last century. Many miners have been killed, and some have been trapped below ground without food, water or light for days, while rescuers from above worked desperately to find them.

In this story, however, it was the miners who were saved, and the people in the town above who waited for rescue. . . .

The Night the Mountain Fell

In 1903 the town of Frank, Alberta, was a noisy mining community. Many of the men slept in tents at night and worked at the coal face during the day. They drifted into town, worked a while, spent their money and drifted out again. Very few records were kept, so nobody knows exactly how many drifters' tents were pitched around town. But neat square houses provided homes for nearly 1000 of Frank's permanent residents. Most of the husbands and fathers worked in the Frank mine too.

The town of Frank, nestled beneath Turtle Mountain, before the slide.

Frank was built at the foot of a large white mountain called Turtle Mountain. Local native people would never camp there. They said that someday the big turtle-shaped triangle of limestone at the top would "nod its head" and roll down the mountain. The townspeople thought that was ridiculous — until April 29, 1903.

On the midnight to 8:00 A.M. "graveyard" shift a small group of men went deep into the mine. One of them noticed that the pit pony, used for pulling ore carts, was nervous. It made him worry about a cave-in, because animals seem to be able to sense such things more easily than people do. But nothing happened, and the men worked busily, hour after hour. In town, things quietened down. The bars closed, and by 4:00 A.M. most of the residents of the town were asleep.

Then it happened. Half of the white mountain high above the town broke loose. A gigantic slab of limestone, the size of a village and weighing about 60 million tonnes, broke apart into boulders as big as houses and buses. These came crashing down the mountainside, crushing and pulverizing everything before them. The homes and other buildings in one whole section of Frank were flattened as if they were made of paper. On and on the boulders bounced and crashed, covering the wide valley floor and rolling halfway up the other side. In just a minute and a half more than a hundred people and their homes or tents were buried under ten storey's-worth of rock.

Right on the edge of the path of destruction

there were houses with one half pulverized and the other still standing. All the people sleeping in one room might be killed, while those in the next would be unharmed. Boards, pipes and roof beams lay scattered with the rocks as far as the eye could see. The Old Man River and the CPR tracks along it lay buried under thirty metres of rock.

A man named Sid Choquette was the hero of the night. He worked for the CPR and knew there was a night train due at any moment. He raced across the hot, broken rocks of the slide and flagged the train down before it reached the area of devastation. If he hadn't succeeded in his desperate effort the train would have crashed straight into the rocks, taking even more lives.

A number of people had lucky escapes. Perhaps the luckiest was Marion Leitch. She was just a baby in a crib when the boulders crushed her house like a cardboard box. She was thrown into the air on impact and would have landed hard, if a pile of hay hadn't landed just moments before she did. She fell onto it as gently as if she had been playfully tossed onto a bed. Marion survived, along with her sisters. But her brothers and parents all perished.

Strangely, the group of on-duty miners escaped. The entrance to the mine was buried under tonnes of rock. The miners dug for hours with their tools, none of them realizing that this was more than a cave-in of the mine entrance. Finally one of the men was pushed out through the hole they had dug. William Warrington stood blinking in the bright sunlight. He stared, unbelieving, at the pile of broken rocks that covered the whole valley. His happiness at escaping the mine's dark trap turned to sorrow when he saw that the rocks covered what had been his home, with his wife and daughters inside.

In the years that followed, the town of Frank was rebuilt a few kilometres away. Nobody wanted to live too close to Turtle Mountain anymore. Today, visitors can see the jumble of rocks stretching across the valley. Beneath, still buried, lie many, many victims of the Frank Slide.

Half of Turtle Mountain broke loose, sending a gigantic slab of limestone, with boulders the size of houses, crashing down the mountainside.

The Disastrous History
of the Springhill Mines

Nova Scotia's "Safest" Mine

Fourteen-year-old Bruce Ryan put on his scratchy mining clothes, stiff and caked with coal dust, took up his lunch and the simple cloth cap that would hold his miner's lamp, and walked the two kilometres from his home to the mine. Bruce had to work. His father was dead and he was taking care of his mother. He wasn't the youngest miner, for the Cumberland Mine in Springhill, Nova Scotia, hired boys as young as twelve.

Ahead, Bruce watched other boys and girls his age walking to school, dressed in clean clothes, carrying books. For a while he had teased the others, bragging to them about working for a living. But secretly he envied them. He never spoke about it, but he was afraid of the mine. Rocks could fall on you. Coal dust or methane gas could ignite with a single spark, sending a wall of fire and an explosive shock wave through all the tunnels of the mine, killing men without warning. Bruce had heard that his mine had recently been inspected and found to be one of the safest in Nova Scotia. Still, Bruce shivered. It was February 21, 1891.

At 12:43 P.M., 580 metres down, a spark from an unknown source ignited airborne coal dust, and an explosion ripped along the east side of one level of tunnels and up to the next level. Its fireball seared the men and boys in its path, killing them instantly. A

A fourteen-year-old worker in a coal mine.

violent shock wave spread everywhere through the maze of tunnels. The miner's lamps blew out. Shouts sounded in the darkness as dazed survivors scrambled to see or to feel their way to the surface.

Bruce Ryan, and younger boys Jospeh Dupee, John Dunn and Willard Carter, died in the mine in those first terrible moments of destruction. Dozens of men were poisoned and died when, stumbling through the darkness, they unknowingly entered the pools of deadly gases called "afterdamp" or "killer damp," formed in low places after a coal mine explosion. Fathers and grandfathers, boys and men: 125 in all were killed that day. It remains the worst mine disaster in Canadian history.

It also remains a great example of selfless heroism. Fourteen-year-old Danny Robertson carried a friend, little Willie Terris, out of the mine on his badly burned back. Ex-miner John Wilson went down without bothering to change from his business clothes and for twenty-four hours helped search the familiar old tunnels for signs of life. Hundreds of off-duty miners put on their equipment and descended into the ruined and gas-filled tunnels to find the survivors. They worked in incredibly dangerous situations, as the wreckage of timbers and equipment and the possibility of another explosion was evident all around them. Many lives were saved by these men and boys who refused to give up hope. Again and again they returned, dragging and carrying half-dead survivors, the blinded, and those crippled in the many rock falls that followed.

News of the terrible disaster spread around the world. Condolences were sent from miners and ordinary folk, from Queen Victoria and from Lord Stanley, the Governor General. Nova Scotia's "safest" mine had turned out to be Canada's most deadly. And it wasn't finished yet.

Fresh Disaster

The mine was repaired and the town of Springhill continued to grow. Boys were no longer allowed to work underground. The men who worked there, the fathers, husbands and sons, tried to keep safe and earn a decent wage.

Sixty-five years after the disaster of 1891, the mine was so deep that it took men more than an hour to get to the coal face. On November 1, 1956, at the Number Four Mine, a train of coal cars being pulled to the surface suddenly broke free. The cars whipped hundreds of metres back down the smooth steel rails until they derailed at great speed, one and a half kilometres down in the mine. When they cut a 2500-volt electrical cable the sparks caused a massive explosion. Along with the blast, walls of flame scorched through many tunnels, killing thirty-two miners and seven more men on the surface. Another eighty-eight men were trapped deep in the lower levels. Nobody knew if they were alive or dead.

Again the mine rescuers hurried in to help. Some were "draegermen," carrying 35-kilogram fresh-air supplies on their backs; others were "barefaced" men, who risked everything to help their friends. Teams of rescuers descended into the scorched mine tunnels. At any moment loose rocks, timbers or sets, barely standing because of the blast, could fall on them. Pockets of poisonous gases could kill them in minutes. But they continued their search, looking for the living among the dead.

Deep in the tunnels, the trapped miners hoped and prayed for a miracle. And it came. After three and a half days, the eighty-eight men were discovered by teams of searchers, and rescued. The survivors became known as the Springhill Miracle.

After this, many people, including the mining company, wanted to close the Springhill mine. But others were anxious that it stay open. There were few enough jobs, and the men couldn't stand the thought of losing their proud though dangerous livelihood. It took another disaster less than three years later to convince them otherwise.

The End of the Springhill Mines

This time it happened at the Number Two Mine, the largest in North America. Its tunnels extended three kilometres deep into the earth, well underneath the ocean floor. On October 23, 1958, at 8:06 P.M. a sudden collapse of ground, called a "bump" by miners, flattened large sections of the mine. Seventy-five miners were killed almost immediately. Off-duty miners and rescue workers from other mines raced to the site. Prepared for all dangers, yet risking their lives, dozens of draegermen descended into the wrecked tunnels. Crawling under groaning timbers, shining their lamps into every crevice that might hide a body, living or dead, they helped seventy-two men escape death during the first night.

Many sections of the mine were totally blocked off and inaccessible, but the draegermen continued to search. Bodies littered the mine and had to be removed carefully and slowly, increasing the agony for those waiting on the surface. Reporters from all parts of Canada and dozens of nations waited with the families at the Number Two Mine. All remembered the "Springhill Miracle" of two and a half years earlier. Would there be another?

After days and days of fruitless searches, hope began to die out and many people felt the searches should end. The draegermen insisted on continuing. And an incredible six and a half days after the bump, twelve desperate but living men were found in a space so small they could only lie flat. One of them had shouted into a pipe just as rescuers passed by the other end of it, many metres away through the rock and rubble.

Word spread that men had been found alive. Two days later still, seven more men were found, trapped but alive, their spirits helped along by the singing of one of them, Maurice Ruddick. Finally, one more man was found in a space no larger than a grave, a miraculous nine days after the collapse.

But, miracle or no miracles, the people of Springhill had had enough of death and disaster. The mines were closed forever.

Slow Death

I worked with 180 men on that job and there's 142 of them in the graveyard.
— *Sammy Byrne, a Newfoundland fluorspar miner*

When the fluorspar mine opened in St. Lawrence, Newfoundland, in 1957, it seemed like a gift from God. Four years of poor catches had left the people of the fishing village sickly, underfed and weak, the children dying of diseases they would otherwise have been able to fight off. The new mine seemed to hold the solution to these problems. Since fluorspar is used in the production of steel and aluminum, there would be a constant demand for the mineral. And although mining would be at least as dangerous as fishing, the work and the pay would be steady all year round.

The fishermen knew nothing about mining, since none of them had ever worked in a mine before. Though there were no regulations about it in Newfoundland at the time, most mines are equipped with two entry shafts, one for the men and ore to get in and out, the other for fresh-air ventilation and, if necessary, emergency escape. There was only one shaft in the St. Lawrence mine. This set-up was cheaper for the mine owners, but dangerous for the miners. The fresh air forced through the single shaft didn't circulate well, and not enough of it reached the miners.

In addition, the men were given "dry hammer"

drills to use. These drills create clouds of dry, choking dust because, unlike "wet" drills, they don't have
water running through the middle of the drill steel.
The miners were unaware that they were working in
one of the dustiest mines in North America. Perhaps
the mine bosses were unaware as well — they
inspected the mine on Sundays, when the dust
would have settled.

And there were serious problems of another sort.
After any blast, dangerous nitrous gases remain for a
while at the blast site. In a mine, miners are instructed to wait half an hour for the gas to clear. But in the
St. Lawrence mine, the bosses ordered the men back
to work as soon as the blast was over. Many of the
men suffered dizzy spells and some would even pass
out for a while.

Experienced miners who came to work at St.
Lawrence from other areas often took one look at
work conditions and quit. But the greatest danger of
all was invisible to even the most experienced miner.
Deadly radiation was leaking from a large deposit of
uranium nearby. Radiation poisoning is terrible, and
can be very subtle: its effects might not be known for
months or even years after exposure. Gradually, one
miner after another sickened with mysterious ail-
ments. Then they began to die.

The sick were sent to a hospital in St. John's, but
seldom were they told what their illnesses were, or
what caused them. But one company doctor did
reveal the truth. Many of the sick men were suffer-
ing from cancer. Others had silicosis, a deadly disease

Miners with well-lubricated drills in a well-ventilated mine.

of the lungs that afflicts miners in particular. Such diseases were caused by the unwholesome conditions of the mine, the doctor explained. Within two weeks he was looking for another job.

In 1960 the Alcan Corporation purchased the mine from its American owners. They dug another shaft to ventilate it properly and replaced the dry hammers with wet drills, and the dust problem diminished. But it was too late for many of the first miners. Disease was already creeping through their bodies. By the early 1970s, one family in three had lost a man.

Many had to go on welfare. Others applied to the company for compensation, but they received so little that they could barely keep their families fed and clothed. The miners couldn't understand why compensation varied from one person to another, according to someone's peculiar scale. What did it matter if a miner was "one-quarter disabled," "half disabled" or "two-thirds disabled"? The issue seemed straightforward to the miners: either a man was disabled, or he wasn't.

Men dying of lung cancer continued to work to earn a few dollars more for their families. Some refused to leave until they barely had enough strength to walk. Others worked until the mine closed in February, 1978.

CHAPTER FIVE

Nature's Fury

The most we can do in the face of nature's fury is prepare for the worst as best we can — and clean up afterward.

The Hurricane That Couldn't Happen

Most Canadians feel they are safe from the weather inside their homes. Thick walls keep out the cold, sealed windows keep out the rain, sturdy foundations hold out the strongest wind.

People living in the southeastern United States or in the Caribbean — hurricane country — know differently. They could have warned the city of Toronto in 1954 how bad it was going to get — if only the unwary Canadians had thought to ask. As it was, eighty-one people were killed and millions of dollars' worth of property was destroyed when Hurricane Hazel came to town.

Hurricane Hazel began near Granada in the Caribbean. It was the eighth hurricane of 1954, and by far the biggest. Its circling winds covered an area 1500 kilometres wide and sent heavy rainfall and screaming winds to the island of Haiti and the American southeast coast. Then, after ten days, it made an unusual hop over the Adirondack Mountains and crossed Lake Ontario, to hit the city of Toronto full force on October 15.

Almost everybody was caught off guard. There had been warnings on the radio, but people thought it just wasn't possible. Hurricanes were for places like Florida, not Toronto.

The hurricane struck near midnight. Its winds weren't as strong as they had been, but it dropped eighteen centimetres of rain in the next twenty-four-hour period, more water than ever before in that period of time. And that was deadly, for already rain had been falling for weeks, and the whole area around Toronto was soggy. The ground was a full sponge. It just couldn't hold any more.

So the billions of litres of water dropped by Hurricane Hazel stayed on the surface, flowing downhill all the time, seeking the lowest places. Each swollen ditch emptied into a racing creek, and each creek poured into a monster river. Each river turned into a raging torrent of brown water with currents so fast that the best swimmers in the world would be swept along like chips of wood. Many of the rivers and creeks were up to three metres deeper than normal. Imagine water from floor to ceiling roaring through a small creek bed!

The first casualties were the bridges, even those built to resist the powerful waters of spring floods. Of the twenty-eight bridges in the affected area, twenty-four were totally wrecked. Next, water began to find its way into houses. Many people woke that Friday night to find their living rooms flooded, water halfway up the stairs. Some didn't even have a chance to leave their beds before the

Part of a house lies tilted onto its side after Hurricane Hazel raged through the city.

water picked their house up off its foundations and floated it along on the incredible currents.

Firefighters and police officers lined the banks and tried to throw ropes to helpless victims standing on houses and cars and in trees. The rising waters reached many before the ropes did, and it wasn't until days later that their bodies were found farther downstream. At one flooded bridge, rescue workers tried to talk a man out of driving his car across. They knew he wouldn't make it. But the man insisted. The car was lifted off the bridge and taken bobbing along on the water, the man and his family screaming for help. They all perished.

The old Bathurst Street bridge at the west bank of the Humber River, after Hurricane Hazel hit.

Eight firefighters were called to rescue people trapped in a car on another street near the Humber River. They hurried to the scene, only to find the people long gone. Then the fire truck itself was caught by the water and the firefighters had to climb on top of it. Nervously they watched the water rise. When it began to roll the fire truck over, the men jumped and tried to swim for shore. Only three of them made it.

In another trouble spot a firefighter named Norm Elwin single-handedly lifted and extended an eleven-metre ladder to desperate flood victims. After the storm, others tried to duplicate his feat. None could: it took at least four men in normal conditions to do what Norm Elwin did alone during the hurricane.

The storm left behind terrible destruction and misery. If a hurricane is predicted for the Toronto area in the future, people who remember Hurricane Hazel may be the first to head for high ground.

Ontario's Black Friday

A generation later, another "impossible" storm landed in an "unlikely" place in Canada. Just after 4:00 P.M. on May 31, 1985, the power went out at the Jellco Packaging plant in Barrie, just north of Toronto. The weather forecast warned of severe thunderstorms and hail; black storm clouds had converged on Barrie and a large part of Central Ontario. One of the plant managers looked at the sky and concluded the power would not be back on soon. He decided to send home the seventy workers who had just arrived for the 4-to-10 evening shift. That decision saved lives.

The violent storm raging over Ontario was spawning one tornado after another, over a huge area. Near Rush Cove on the Bruce Peninsula, far to the northwest of Barrie, the deadly spout of one tornado had spun down to the earth and begun to wander, aimless but destructive, like the finger of an idle giant. Then another tornado formed in Egremont Township, and travelled northeastward, leaving behind it an eighty-five-kilometre-long path of wasted farmland, splintered trees and flattened buildings. Yet another, the longest-running tornado on record, went from Arthur, Ontario, to the farming district of Holland Marsh, a distance of ninety kilometres. More tornadoes formed until by the end of the afternoon at least nine separate tornadoes had been sighted.

In Orangeville, about eighty kilometres southwest of Barrie, an entire plaza was wrecked in less than a minute. All fifteen stores were flattened, but miraculously nobody was killed.

On a nearby street, unaware of what was happening, eighteen-year-old Debbie Molto tried to close her front door: "The wind was so strong I was pulled out onto the porch and I couldn't get back into the house. I was crouching down, I think. The noise was terrific. I got soaked in the driving rain and I remember seeing lots of hail and lightning. I wasn't really sure what was happening. Then the clouds disappeared and the sun came out. I was still in a daze and I was covered in mud and bits of fibreglass insulation."

Debbie walked to her neighbour's house across the street and commented on the damage to the woman's house. The neighbour said, "Look at your house." Debbie turned, and saw for the first time that most of the roof was gone.

Near Orangeville, Harold and Bruce Wilson's beef cattle farm took a direct hit by one of the tornadoes. Harold and Bruce escaped with their lives, as did most of their cattle. But almost all the buildings were destroyed and seventeen of their eighteen farm vehicles were reduced to junk, including two ten-tonne trucks. In moments, much of the work of the last thirty years was undone. Their loss, estimated at $1.5 million, was probably one of the greatest ever claimed by an individual farmer.

But in Barrie, a pleasant city of 45 000 people, a large tornado was doing the worst damage of all. This tornado, as randomly destructive as all the others, was heading for a major highway, factories and houses. Motorists were paralyzed with fear as their cars and trucks were lifted, flipped over or rammed into other vehicles. Jellco Industries was flattened into a pile of twisted metal beams and knife-edged pieces of sheet metal. Had the workers been there, certainly death would have been there too. On nearby Adelaide Street, most of the houses were completely destroyed in a few moments of furious wind. Later, photos of this area would be seen in newspapers all over North America. It looked like a war zone.

Eight people died in Barrie as the result of that tornado, but many rescuers and emergency aid workers agreed that the death toll could have been much higher: if the electrical power had been on, deadly fires would certainly have followed in the aftermath. In the smaller communities surrounding Barrie, people ran to cellars to escape the deadly funnel clouds, which most eyewitnesses said sounded like freight trains passing by. Luckily most of the destruction was to trees, crops and property, not people. But still, four people died in the various tornadoes which rampaged the small towns and cities of central Ontario, bringing the death toll to twelve that Friday afternoon. One hundred million dollars' worth of damage was done in about an hour.

But from all sides, help appeared. In cities like Barrie, disaster plans were put into effect by city officials, police, hospital and fire department workers. Volunteers from a ham radio club provided commu-

A Barrie sign lies demolished in the wake of the violent tornado. (Bruno Favero)

nication, since most of the phone lines had been ripped apart. The Red Cross organized the various volunteer groups. Chaos turned to order as the people began the grim task of helping the wounded and finding those trapped in the rubble. Three hundred members of a nearby Mennonite community came daily for weeks, helping to tear down and remove the mess of broken building materials which had once been homes.

The clean-up lasted for months, but the rebuilding was completed in a surprisingly short time. Today, there are hardly any traces of the tornadoes of 1985. But people have not forgotten. The likelihood of another tornado returning to Barrie is very slim, yet parents are particularly careful to instruct their children in what to do if another tornado comes: if you are at home, go to the basement. If you are in a building without a basement, stay away from the windows and crouch low beside an inside wall. If you are outside, lie down in a ditch or other low place.

The Regina Cyclone

Long ago, the people of Regina, Saskatchewan, had been surprised by their own, even more unlikely tornado. It was June 30, 1912, and the city was very young. No one knew what it meant when two dark clouds collided over the Queen City. But by the end of that Dominion Day weekend, many people had learned — the hard way.

The tornado formed above Wascana Lake, and first sucked the water up into a long green spout. Several boaters were drawn up with the water and killed. One, however, had a miraculous escape. The thirteen-year-old boy was picked up in his canoe and spun through the air for over a kilometre, only to land gently, far from the water, with nothing worse than a broken arm.

Then the tornado moved on, across the land. People, houses and horses were lifted into the dark funnel and whirled around at speeds of more than 100 kilometres an hour. In the peculiar way of tornadoes, in some places buildings on one side of a street were totally destroyed while those on the other merely lost their windows. Some buildings lost just the walls on one side, revealing the interiors of offices and apartments to anyone who cared to look. Surprised people were suddenly exposed to the world, sitting down to dinner or even taking a bath. Three large churches were completely destroyed. A fourth was left unharmed — the only one with people in it.

Regina after the devastating tornado locals called the "Regina Cyclone."

Most of the windows of the new Saskatchewan Legislative Building were blown out and much of its copper roof was sent flying off into the prairie. The examination papers for all the province's public schools had been stacked neatly on tables in one of the exposed offices. As if in answer to students' prayers, the tornado scattered the papers like leaves on a fall day. No one in Saskatchewan had to write final exams that year.

Just as suddenly as it began, the tornado left the city and disappeared. A young woman who went outside just after the storm ended remarked on the silence. Those trapped or wounded hardly made a sound. Instead they waited quietly to be rescued. There was even some good-natured joking as people lay piled on top of each other in dark basements or under the remains of stores or apartments.

Slowly the extent of the damage became clear. Here was the roof of a house. Fifty metres away was one of its outside walls. On one street a bed, hardly rumpled, sat waiting to be claimed. Its owner lived three blocks away. There was amazing evidence of the fierce power of the storm. Grass straws had been hurled through the air so hard that they were found embedded in tree trunks. Boards had smashed into brick walls with such force that they stuck out like porcupine quills. And of course, many people had been killed and hundreds were left wounded and trapped.

Yet there were also many miraculous escapes. A boy desperately tried to hold onto his baby sister while their house collapsed around them, but she was torn from his arms. Later she was found in the oven of the kitchen stove, with only a few bruises on her legs. A woman and her baby fell through two floors of their house and landed in the basement, completely unhurt. In one office building a book-keeper had been using the holiday to catch up on his work. He went into the company vault to get some ledgers and when he came out he found the building had collapsed all around him. On a street corner a rooster was crowing as loudly as he could. All his feathers were missing except those on his tail.

Rebuilding the city began immediately. Repairs to the essential services were the first priority. The province lent money, and many nearby cities gave tents and lumber to help the people who had lost their homes. Officers of the Royal North-West Mounted Police were called in to stand guard over the valuables and furniture that lay scattered all over the city. Military troops and Boy Scouts were also called in to help in whatever ways they could.

The people of Regina called their tornado a cyclone, but that word really refers to hurricanes and typhoons. It was a tornado, and each year such storms occur farther and farther north . . . so that the possibility of another gets stronger all the time.

Edmonton's Black Friday

The last week of July in 1987 had been a long, sweltering one in Edmonton. On Friday, July 31, thunderclouds rolling across the big sky of the prairie promised rain and relief from the heat. People eagerly looked forward to the weekend, many of them preparing for trips to the cottage, or for camping. But many would not make it out that weekend.

Tom Taylor was leaving his pharmacy in a plaza south of Edmonton, when he noticed a long thin funnel descend from one of the black storm clouds scudding northward. Fascinated, he watched it touch a farmer's field and turn black with the dirt lifted hundreds of metres up into its swirling funnel. It was a small tornado, perhaps only ten metres wide, but still dangerous. He phoned the weather office, giving the first warning.

The black storm cloud moved toward Beaumont, just outside of Edmonton. Here again the deadly cloud touched down, but now it was ten times wider and much more destructive, with a sound like a dozen freight trains. The furious black funnel spun wickedly, carving out destruction. Steadily it twisted northward, leaving forty kilometres of wreckage behind it: bits of houses, trees, cars and the broken lives of both people and animals.

The hardest hit area was the Evergreen Trailer Park. More than 91 of the 600 trailer homes there were completely mangled and another hundred were badly damaged. Fifteen people lost their lives in the Evergreen Trailer Park. Some authorities were amazed the death toll was not higher.

Among the dead were four members of one family, Marvin Reimer and three of his children, Dianne and twins Dawn and Darcy. Another woman, Kelly Pancel, hugged her one-month-old baby to protect her from the storm. The baby survived, but Kelly died, her life given for her child. Many were injured by the broken bits of trailers and furniture whipping around them in dizzying circles. Residents like Mark Ernewein and his wife, who had been away shopping, considered themselves lucky to be alive even though their home and all their furniture was completely ripped apart.

An industrial area called Refinery Row looked like a battle zone after the tornado ripped through it. Twelve workers died as large steel factory roofs collapsed and cars and trucks were tossed like toys. Sixty businesses were seriously damaged or destroyed in a few minutes of insane, storm-driven violence.

But there were miracles too. The tornado passed through the Clareview neighbourhood where Rod and Mary Grandish had their home. Mary was busy packing for the weekend camping trip, and remembers that strange and terrifying half-hour:

"It got very dark and the streetlights came on. Through the front window I noticed our travel trailer being pulled across the driveway. Then the neighbour's garden shed landed in our yard and I knew we were in trouble. There was a sound like a jet plane. I went to the back door and as I watched, our garage was lifted right off the foundations and then it folded up and turned sideways. It collapsed in a heap. Then the roof of the house caved in and I thought we were going to die."

Mary ran for her three-month-old son, Cody, but his room was gone. So was his crib. There was nothing left. Her friend Ron Madarash joined her in searching for the baby in the lashing wind and rain, Mary all the while thinking, "A tornado has taken my son." Finally, in the remains of the master bedroom, they saw two little sleeper-clad feet sticking out from the wreckage.

"I was so worried at first, because he was so quiet and he was bleeding. I could tell he was still alive but I didn't know how badly hurt he was. I kissed him and prayed he would be okay," says Mary. At the hospital, Cody was examined and treated for his injuries — miraculously, minor ones that soon healed.

Hospitals were ready for patients like Cody, and worse. Emergency response plans in the City of Edmonton and Strathcona County sprang into place. Teams of volunteers helped the police keep order and transport victims to the hospital. Gas company employees shut down gas lines and electricians shut down power to prevent explosions or fires. There were a few, put out by the several fire departments involved; then firefighters helped search for trapped people and rubble-buried bodies. Even pets were cared for by animal control officials.

A tornado darkens the sky over Edmonton on "Black Friday." (Robert den Hartigh)

Amazingly, despite the destruction of over 300 homes and many factories, looting was almost unheard of, with only one person being arrested during the first ten days.

The chances of a tornado of that size and destructive power hitting a major city are always slim. Nevertheless, most cities and towns regularly prepare for such emergencies, drilling their hospital staff, firefighters, police and ambulance crews until their response to catastrophe is automatic and well organized. The Alberta government learned what they could from Edmonton's Black Friday, studying their emergency response procedure and making plans to improve it. But this is small return from an experience that cost 27 irreplaceable lives, 300 painful injuries and an estimated $330 million worth of property damage, the highest in Alberta's history.

Of Canadian tornadoes, only the Regina Cyclone of 1912 was worse.

CHAPTER SIX

Disasters on the Move

Every day, all of us risk our lives, often without giving it a second's thought. How? We step onto a bridge, artfully suspended above a churning river. We hop onto a bus or train, and go hurtling along at breathtaking speeds. We board a plane, and sip cola and nibble snacks with nothing but cold air and clouds as far as the eye can see. Why? Because we trust the things we have made, and the people that operate them, to do what they are supposed to do.

And sometimes, our trust is betrayed. Perhaps it was a design flaw, or a simple, ghastly mistake. Perhaps someone should have spoken out, but kept silent; or even worse, kept silent because the disaster was maliciously planned. Perhaps the cause will forever be a mystery. . . .

The Hinton Train Wreck

In the early morning hours of February 8, 1986, passengers of the VIA Rail Supercontinental Number Four were just getting up to have breakfast. Outside, the beautiful and cold Alberta scenery whipped by at over seventy-eight kilometres an hour. The train was heading eastward, leaving Jasper and the Rocky Mountains and rolling on to Edmonton. In the glass-domed dining car the view of the foothills was tremendous.

This passenger train was fourteen cars long, with

two locomotives in the lead and one in the middle. It was actually two trains joined together, one from Prince Rupert and the other from Vancouver. Like all trains on the Canadian National lines, this one was being monitored by computers hundreds of kilometres away. The latest in safety equipment, radios and signals was a virtual guarantee of safety for passengers and cargo, night or day. One hundred and fifteen people were on board.

Then it happened. The VIA Rail train rounded a slight bend seventeen kilometres east of Hinton. Passengers in the dome car were stunned to see a CN freight train coming toward them, at almost a hundred kilometres per hour. There were only nineteen seconds to impact, hardly enough time to even begin to slow a train down. The brakes went untouched — perhaps the crew of the passenger train were frozen in fear. A pause, and then . . .

The two trains collided. The freight train, forty times heavier than the passenger train and pulled by three powerful locomotives, plowed on through the passenger train like a boulder through a cardboard box. Fuel from the colliding locomotives spilled everywhere and burst into roaring flame. The VIA train's two lead locomotives, its baggage car and the leading day coach were completely destroyed. Car after car behind them was derailed and flung sideways into a growing heap. And still the freight train kept coming, almost two kilometres of it; car after car ramming into the mess, leaping, spinning and catapulting over the others.

Twisted debris litters the track after a collision between a passenger train and a freight train near Hinton, Alberta, in 1986. The crash killed twenty-three people. (Canadian Press EDMS)

Survivors could not describe the devastation they saw. It was beyond words. Heaps of wheat, broken passenger cars, steel pipes as long as two houses, flaming diesel engines and punctured tanks of toxic liquids were strewn everywhere. Smoke from the fires stained the clear mountain sky. Twenty-three people were killed, including the head-end crews of both trains, eighteen passengers in the VIA Rail day coach, and one passenger in the dome car.

Many of those were killed by fire. But others were saved. A grain car spilled onto one of the day coaches and smothered the flames there. And months later, the Commission of Inquiry heard of many acts of heroism performed by passengers and the surviving crew members.

But how did this accident come to be?

CN freight train Number 413 had been heading westward. Much of the track in the area was single track, so the freight train's task was to switch to the nearest sideline when an eastbound passenger train was approaching, to wait until it had passed by. It was a simple routine, one the crew performed thousands of times over the years. The train had switched to the stretch of double track east of Hinton. Ahead was a yellow-over-red train signal that meant the train should prepare to stop.

It rolled on by at full power. Neither of the two men in the front locomotive made an attempt to stop. The conductor in the caboose did not radio the front end crew about the missed signal.

Another signal four kilometres ahead showed

three red lights: "stop and wait." The freight train flew past the red signals as if they didn't exist, still at the same rate of speed, which was already fifteen kilometres an hour too fast. By now it was broad daylight; clear and sunny weather. Farther ahead was the switch, set to allow the passenger train through on the main line. The freight train jumped the switch and continued to roll westward, but now on the main line, with the passenger train up ahead, unseen around a bend, heading toward it.

Computers at the CN yards sensed the trespassing of the freight train and changed the signals facing the passenger train to red. But it was already too late. Each of the trains was moving much too quickly to stop in time. They were doomed.

Much later, a study by Justice René Foisy decided that the safety equipment had been working perfectly, and put the blame on the CN freight train crew. But there were still many unknown facts. The engineer in the CN locomotive was known to be in poor health. Had he suffered a heart attack? The brakeman, the second man in the cab, had the flu, and neither of the men had had much sleep in the last twenty hours. Were they sleeping then?

When all else fails, trains have a "deadman's pedal," which is supposed to sound a whistle and apply the brakes automatically if the engineer falls asleep or becomes unconscious and his foot comes off the pedal. But for some unknown reason even this last safety device failed to prevent the tragedy on that cold Alberta morning.

Fire or Ice?

Into the early morning dew of December 12, 1985, a DC-8 aircraft thundered down the runway and rose into the air after refuelling at Newfoundland's Gander airport. Loaded with American soldiers returning from duty in the Middle East, the Arrow Air jet began climbing for its final destination, Fort Campbell, Kentucky. The servicemen, exhausted from the long flight and months of peacekeeping duty, were going home for Christmas. But just moments after the flight began, the jet crashed, exploding into pieces. All 256 people on board were killed.

Dead soldiers and flight crew, smouldering aircraft wreckage and the remains of the luggage were scattered widely. Christmas presents, clothing, souvenirs from the Middle East littered the ground, heartbreaking bits and pieces of so many lives brought suddenly to an end. Searchers, arriving on the scene within minutes, found only a sickening mess — not one sign of life.

It was the worst aircraft crash ever for the American military. For years it was listed among the top ten crashes in the world. But there has been more anger and doubt raised by this crash than by any in recent memory. Many investigators and the families of many of the dead feel that the mystery of this aircraft disaster has never been fully solved.

An extremist terrorist group claimed responsibility for the crash, saying they had planted a bomb. In fact, many eyewitnesses told of seeing flames coming from the underside of the aircraft as it passed over their heads. One described the flames as bright enough to read by. Another eyewitness saw the jet explode before it hit the ground. These things would suggest that, indeed, a bomb had gone off — or at least, that there was a fire in one of the engines.

Twenty of the soldiers were from a special anti-terrorist group and were possible targets for the attack. Mysterious wooden crates had been loaded when the aircraft was in Egypt. The crates were not part of any soldier's luggage. The airline was later identified as being one among several used to smuggle weapons to enemies of the Americans. The first at the crash scene, police and firefighters, heard many smaller explosions that sounded like ammunition going off. These factors suggest that this was no ordinary jet crash.

But investigations done by the Canadian and U.S. governments blamed the pilot for this crash. The official investigation decided that the aircraft had crashed because of wing icing, a dangerous condition in which ice buildup changes the shape of the upper wing surface and disturbs its "lift." However, the pilot, Captain John Griffin, was a very careful man with years of flying experience in all kinds of weather. Would he really have risked his plane and the lives in his care by taking off with ice on his wings? He, the co-pilot and the ground crew, men with over thirty years experience, had all looked for and not found any evidence of ice.

An RCMP officer examines the wreckage of the Arrow Air DC-8 jetliner December 13, 1985, the day after it

When another American jet was blown up by terrorist bombs over Lockerbie, Scotland, the wreckage was carefully examined for months after. In the Arrow Air case, a top American general arrived on the crash scene just a few days after and ordered that bulldozers cover the remains. Investigators hired by the families of the dead soldiers thought the crash more likely to have been caused by a bomb than wing ice. But they may never know for sure.

The Mysterious Crash of Flight 831

On November 29, 1963, a Trans-Canada Airlines jet dove into a hillside at Ste. Thérèse-de-Blainville in Quebec, instantly killing all 118 people on board.

Flight 831 was a routine one, filled with business passengers flying to Toronto at suppertime. It was raining hard, and eight would-be passengers cursed the traffic delays that made them miss their flight. They would soon be blessing them instead. The regular pilot was late flying into Montreal as well, so Captain John Snider took his place. Snider knew as much about the big DC-8 as any pilot in the world. The co-pilot and the flight engineer were also well acquainted with the comparatively new jet. But all their combined knowledge and experience couldn't save them that rainy Friday night.

The plane's four jet engines pushed it up into the rainstorm, each engine gulping down jet fuel and air and blasting out 8000 kilos of thrust. At 1000 metres, the co-pilot reported to Dorval that everything was as it should be. But something happened before the plane reached 2000 metres, the next regular check-in point. It might have been a powerful air current, or perhaps a faulty instrument in the cockpit. No one knows why, but for some reason the fifty-metre-long aircraft was suddenly diving for the ground at full speed.

When a jet as large as a DC-8 goes into a dive, it reaches such high speeds so quickly that thousands of metres are needed to slow the plane and bring it up. It can't be done too quickly, or the plane's wings will be torn off. Flight 831 was not high enough. With insufficient altitude and time, the pilots did the best they could. But the jet screamed into a hillside, killing all aboard. The impact shook the ground so hard that people living nearby wondered if they were experiencing an earthquake.

A column of smoke led people to the area of the crash. All they found were a few pieces of twisted metal. Today, specially built machines encased in strong, crash-proof boxes constantly record the movements and sounds of an aircraft and its crew. But in 1963 flight recorders weren't required in Canadian aircraft, so no one knows what happened in those few final seconds. The secret of this crash lies with the dead.

Investigators search through the wreckage of the doomed DC-8.

Bridging the Gap

Bridges may last for a century, and we cross them with hardly a thought about our safety. But the men and women who build them know that it is during construction that they are most likely to fall. Before the final coat of paint is on them, bridges will show their strengths or their weaknesses. . . .

The Nightmare That Almost Came True

On the night of June 16, 1958, Gary Poirier had a nightmare. He dreamed that the bridge he was working on collapsed, and he was cut in half by a steel cable as he fell. The next morning Gary was nervous when he went to work on the new Second Narrows Bridge in Vancouver. Like the old bridge it was replacing, it would join the city of Vancouver to North Vancouver on the other side of Burrard Inlet.

It was a warm and sunny day, and the other high-steel construction workers were in a good mood, walking back and forth on steel beams just fifteen centimetres wide. The section of the bridge Gary was working on was a long span hanging out over the water of the Inlet. Like the other workers, Gary wore a bright yellow life jacket. A man in a rowboat below was poised to rescue anyone who might accidentally fall.

Gary tried to forget his dream, but he couldn't. Suddenly, at 3:40 P.M., there were two loud cracks, like rifle shots, and the farthest span, the one Gary was working on, dropped toward the water. Some of

The Second Narrows Bridge collapsed, killing eighteen people.

the men hung on with all their strength. Others jumped, pushing themselves out as far as they could from the falling steel.

The whole span fell about fifteen storeys before plunging into the water. It pulled a concrete pillar out of place, sending the next span and the men working on it crashing down as well. Some plunged through the water to the bottom, weighed down by their heavy tool belts. Others were pinned underneath the steel beams and killed. Still others rode the girders down like cowboys, jumping off at the right moment. Gary fell exactly as he had in his dream, but he wasn't cut in half. He was one of the lucky ones who lived.

Boats came from everywhere to help rescue the men, some of whom had to be cut free from the twisted wreckage. George Schmidt landed on top of a steel girder just above the water. When he noticed that one of his legs had been cut off below the knee, he calmly tied his work belt around it to stop the bleeding, lit a cigarette and waited. "Thanks, fellas," was all he said when he was picked up.

Eighteen people died in the collapse. Work went on, and the Second Narrows Bridge opened two years later, in 1960. One of the survivors cut the ribbon. An investigation later claimed that the accident was the result of a mathematical error. But the two engineers who are thought to have made the mistake are among the eighteen dead, so their story can never be told.

The Bridge That Fell Twice

In the year 1900, a group of businessmen from Quebec organized the construction of a bridge across the St. Lawrence River near their city. They chose a particular American company, trusting its expertise to get the job done. The job would get done, but not before being the scene of two major disasters.

The company designed a long, elegant bridge, the longest cantilever bridge in the world. A cantilever bridge is one which is balanced in long sections on few pillars. The design for this particular bridge, however, was flawed. Theodore Cooper, the chief engineer, knew this, but he chose to keep quiet. He thought that the bridge, though weak, would still be strong enough for the job. A lot of people were excited about the project, and Cooper was worried that if he pointed out the flaws in the design he wouldn't get another opportunity to be involved in the construction of something so magnificent. The chance for a grand finish to his proud career would be lost. He approved the plans, and the construction of the bridge began.

John Splicer was a high-steel construction worker, one of the best. He was a man from the Kahnawake Reserve near Montreal. The men of his band were famous for their fearlessness and skill while working in high places, and they should have felt at ease working on the new bridge.

But they did not. John and his friends worried constantly about chord A-9-L, one of the bridge's heavy vertical steel beams. There was a bend in it that grew noticeably worse each day. The foremen and engineers on the job tried to have the chord bolted and riveted back straight, but it didn't work. The bend only increased.

Now the engineers were alarmed. In August, 1907, one of them went to New York to discuss the situation with Theodore Cooper. Cooper realized the weakness in the design was showing after all, and ordered that work on the bridge be stopped immediately. But it was too late. On August 27, before the engineer could return to Quebec with the news, the bridge collapsed.

John Splicer wasn't on the bridge that day. He had stayed home, too nervous to go to work. But many of his lifelong friends had reported for duty as usual. Several were still on the bridge when, right around quitting time, chord A-9-L finally gave in to the stress and bent around like a pretzel. In less than a second, support wires and beams snapped loose and the whole structure fell. It dropped fifty metres before it came to rest in a twisted tangle of metal.

Half of the bridge fell into the muddy waters of the river, crushing or drowning those who were unable to spring away in time. Rescuers rushed in, but there was little they could do for the men trapped in the wreckage. There wasn't enough time to set up cutting torches before the waters of the St. Lawrence began to rise with the tide, and they could only watch helplessly as the men drowned one by one. Of the seventy-five workers who died that day,

The elegant bridge was reduced to this in a few short seconds.

thirty-five were from John Splicer's reserve. It was the worst bridge-building disaster in the world.

The project was not abandoned, however. Nine years later, in 1916, a stronger and better-designed bridge was almost completed. The last piece, the centre section, was being hoisted from barges floating on the river when, suddenly, a chunk of steel broke off and the whole section fell. Thirteen men perished.

Now everyone was nervous. Some claimed the bridge was cursed. Nevertheless, on September 20, 1917, apprehensive workmen finally lifted and bolted into place a new centre section. The Quebec Bridge was finished at last, eighty-nine lives and seventeen years after it was begun.

Many have forgotten the story behind this bridge. But there are two groups of Canadians who will always remember it. The high-steel workers of the Kahnawake Reserve near Montreal is one group. After the collapse of 1907, band elders made the men promise never again to work all together on one project.

The professional engineers of Canada is the other. This disaster showed that even well-trained professionals have to be on their guard. When engineers graduate from McGill University in Montreal, part of the graduation ceremony is conducted in a room encircled by one of the large steel chains used in building the disastrous bridge. And it is said that the iron rings that all Canadian engineers wear originally came from a Quebec Bridge girder — a daily reminder of what terrible losses can come from engineering mistakes.

Another Terrible Mistake

Landing any plane, large or small, is the most difficult part of flying. Many things must be done in the right order and smoothly, and all in a very short time.

Landing commercial passenger jets is particularly difficult. They touch down at high speed, then have to slow down very quickly to avoid overshooting the runway. To help with this, they are equipped with large flaps on the wings called spoilers. When up, these create powerful drag, slowing the aircraft and "spoiling" the ability of the wings to lift it. They are designed to be used after the aircraft has touched the runway. If they are put in operation while the plane is still in the air they can cause it to drop like a dead bird.

On the DC-8 of the early 1970s, the spoilers were operated by a two-way lever. The co-pilot would do one of two things: push the lever just before landing, in which case the flaps would open automatically the moment the wheels touched the runway; or go the manual route and pull the lever at the moment of touchdown, opening the flaps instantly.

Naturally, the co-pilot had to remember to push the spoiler control-lever, not pull it, while the jet was still in the air. Think how often you pull a door, when the sign right in front of you says PUSH. It's a simple mistake, isn't it? But in a plane, it's fatal.

On May 5, 1970, an Air Canada DC-8 was land-

The DC-8 and all its passengers and crew — 109 lives — were lost because of a simple mistake. (David Davies)

ing at Pearson International Airport in Toronto, then called Malton Airport. The pilot, Pete Hamilton, and the co-pilot were busy in the cockpit with the rapid sequence of landing procedures. When the plane was fifteen metres above the runway, the co-pilot reached for the spoiler control-lever. Instead of *pushing* it into automatic mode, he *pulled* it into manual mode, opening the spoilers too soon.

The aircraft dropped immediately and flopped onto the runway, the right wing smacking into the ground. The flight recorder registered the pilot shouting, "No! No! No!" and the co-pilot saying, "Sorry! Oh, sorry, Pete."

Hamilton decided to take off and fly around again, not knowing one of the engines had been ripped off and jet fuel was pouring out of the right wing. The jet did gain height and started to circle around. But then, suddenly, there were three mighty explosions. The entire right wing fell away and the jet plummeted into a farmer's field, killing all 109 people aboard.

In 1971, an American pilot made the very same error while on a training flight. Fortunately he was still able to land the plane safely and nobody was hurt. Then, in 1973, an Icelandic Airlines DC-8 co-pilot again pulled the lever instead of pushing it. The crash was not fatal, but there were passengers who were badly hurt. It is strongly suspected that the same mistake was responsible for the crash of a Japan Airlines DC-8 in Moscow in 1972.

After years of such errors, the system for operating the spoilers on DC-8s was changed. But the change was made too late for the ill-fated 109 passengers and crew of Air Canada Flight 621.

A Week of Fear

Sometimes accidents happen. And sometimes, miracles occur. When the two come together, you thank your lucky stars, clean up, and learn what you can.

Near midnight on Saturday, November 10, 1979, a freight train rolled steadily through quiet Mississauga, Ontario. It was over a kilometre long and carried a dangerous cargo, including toluene (a highly flammable liquid), propane and chlorine gas. Slowly it rumbled past houses full of sleeping people.

It passed factories and highrise apartment buildings, and people slept on. But dogs and cats awoke and listened to sounds human ears couldn't detect: a protesting, high-pitched squeal. Something was very wrong with this train. An axle on one of the cars wasn't getting any oil. It had become what railway workers call a "hot box."

With no oil to cool it, it got so hot that it began to glow. Finally the friction and heat became too great, and the ailing axle and its wheels broke off and rolled into a quiet backyard. A tank car containing toluene, now missing two wheels, dragged on down the track, pushed along by the many heavy cars behind it. In places the dragging car snapped the sturdy railroad ties like toothpicks. Flames danced in the darkness, but because of the many bends and curves in the track the engineer and brakeman at the front of the train couldn't see what was going on.

Then, at Mavis Road crossing, the tank car

slipped sideways and finally came off the track. The cars behind rammed into it with enormous force, and in seconds there was a giant zigzag of tank cars lying crumpled together on the tracks. The engineer knew there was a problem only when the automatic brakes locked on the front cars, dragging the powerful diesel engines to a halt.

Larry Krupa, the brakeman, went back along the line. He was in the process of releasing the brakes when the flames ignited a tank car and turned it into an exploding missile that rocketed through the air, missing him by less than a hundred metres.

The derailment had taken place in one of the very few places in Mississauga where there is an open space around the railway tracks, the first of many miracles to be seen that long week in November. Had the car derailed a minute earlier or later, it would have been beside apartment buildings or houses, and the exploding cars would have killed many people. As it was, the ball of flame from the first exploded tank car was seen for several kilometres, and people in nearby Toronto and Oakville heard it, and felt the impact.

Firefighters rushed to the scene and set up hoses to spray the wrecked tank cars. They were constantly sprinting for cover, as the cars kept exploding and shooting through the air. By another miracle, none of the cars landed near the firefighters or other emergency workers on the scene.

It soon became known that one of the tank cars contained chlorine gas. Liquid chlorine is used in

Deadly fumes spilled from the hole in this chlorine tanker. (Frank Calleja)

swimming pools and household products. Chlorine gas was used as a weapon during World War I: its yellowish-green cloud would creep along the ground and choke soldiers in their trenches. In that derailed tank, there was enough chlorine gas to kill a whole army — or a city.

The heads of the police and fire departments, the Mississauga mayor and many other emergency workers were on the scene quickly. Mississauga's emergency response plan was kicked into action. Police Chief Burroughs gave the evacuation orders. Deep sleepers were ordered awake, and out of their homes. Within an hour the area was deserted. People went to friends and relatives or to emergency shelters that were quickly set up in schools and shopping malls.

At the scene of the accident, firefighters sweated in the heat while small amounts of leaking chlorine gas and other chemicals made their eyes smart and water. They used hoses to cool off the fire and hoped much of the propane and other flammable chemicals would burn off.

Then the wind direction changed, and with the change came a new order to evacuate. Another section of Mississauga was cleared of people, and the emergency shelters were even more crowded. Experts in handling chlorine spills were rushed to the scene, but they were unable to suggest a way to patch the leaking tank car. All attempts to plug the hole failed.

Yet another section of Mississauga was evacuated.

In all, nearly a quarter of a million people had to leave their homes during the emergency. Some were unable to return for six days. Volunteer workers and police patrolled the streets and kept unauthorized people out. Others watered plants and fed animals the anxious residents had been forced to leave behind.

Eventually heavy-duty air bags were used to plug the hole in the leaking tank car. The chlorine gas was mixed with caustic soda to make it harmless, and the people of Mississauga were allowed to return to their homes. So ended the biggest evacuation in North America, all without a single loss of life: another miracle.

Trains like the one that derailed in Mississauga pass through Canadian towns and cities every day. Each year about 300 trains derail in Canada, but most of them go off the track in lonely, faraway places. Even so, government studies are recommending that trains carrying dangerous chemicals be watched especially carefully, and that tank cars containing chlorine and other poisons be painted bright colours so they can be easily identified if there is a wreck.

An Act of Hatred

Terrorism. How can people be so full of hate that they are willing to kill hundreds of innocents to make a point?

On June 22, 1985, at Vancouver International Airport, a man bought a one-way ticket from Vancouver to New Delhi, India. The last part of the flight would be on an Air Canada jumbo jet. He gave a suitcase to the clerk, took his ticket and quietly disappeared in the crowd. The suitcase contained a bomb. Hours earlier another man had placed a similar suitcase on a flight destined for Tokyo, Japan, also on an Air India jumbo jet. He did not get on board either. The men were part of an organization which hated the government of India. These terrorists were so full of hatred they were willing to kill hundreds of innocent passengers.

Air India Flight 003 landed without incident at Narita International Airport in Tokyo, fourteen minutes ahead of schedule. The luggage was being removed from the aircraft when, at 3:19 P.M., two baggage handlers were blown to pieces and four others were seriously hurt when the suitcase bomb went off. If the plane had been on schedule, rather than fourteen minutes early, 390 people would probably have died.

Forty-five minutes later the other Air India flight, 182, a Boeing 747, was flying over the Atlantic ocean heading toward London, England. The mood had been cheerful as families in Toronto gathered at the airport to say goodbye to beloved sons, daughters, husbands and wives leaving for vacation or business in India. Most of the families, now Canadian citizens, had come to Canada years earlier and were returning to visit relatives in India. The plane had stopped briefly in Montreal to pick up more passengers. All was well.

The pilots had just contacted the air traffic control centre in Shannon, Ireland. Then, 200 kilometres from the coast of Ireland and without warning, the bomb suddenly exploded, ripping apart the aluminum skin of the huge jet. One can only imagine the terror as the jumbo jet separated into several large pieces and spilled many passengers into the air, still travelling forward at hundreds of kilometres per hour. The remains of the aircraft and the bodies of the passengers plunged almost five kilometres to the ocean below and hit the water with incredible force. For any who may have survived the fall, the impact was fatal. Parts of the airplane scattered and sank quickly, taking almost 200 bodies to the endless dark of the ocean floor.

The pilots hadn't had time even to cry out, but Shannon air traffic control knew something was wrong. There were six seconds of a silent signal from the jet, indicating a microphone was open. Then the Boeing 747 disappeared from their screens. Other aircraft following the same flight plan were contacted but could not see it.

Search and rescue teams from Ireland, Canada and Britain came as soon as they could, but found only bodies, empty life jackets and some luggage scattered over the ocean in a wide area. The people of Cork, Ireland, opened their hearts to grieving families as 131 bodies were brought in from the crash site. With simple caring words and acts of kindness, Irish citizens and military and hospital officials helped the relatives deal with their first hours of grief.

It was soon clear to investigators that a bomb had caused the crash. They were sure it was connected to the bomb at Narita airport. Investigators from Canada, Ireland and India sent small submarines deep down to the wreck of the Air India 747 site in the Irish Sea. Seven hundred kilograms of wreckage were recovered. Japanese investigators worked patiently for many days over the tiniest fragments of the bomb. They learned that it had been concealed in a portable radio, and using pieces that showed its serial and model numbers, traced it to a small town in British Columbia.

In time, Canadian investigators were able to narrow their investigation to a few suspects, but could not find enough proof to arrest any of the terrorists involved. A prime suspect, Talwinder Singh Parmar, was shot and killed by police while resisting arrest in India in October of 1992.

The bloody bombing of Flight 182 is the deadliest terrorist attack in Canada. Nothing can bring back the lives of so many innocent Canadians who died so suddenly. Many of them were promising young teens, talented children of successful parents,

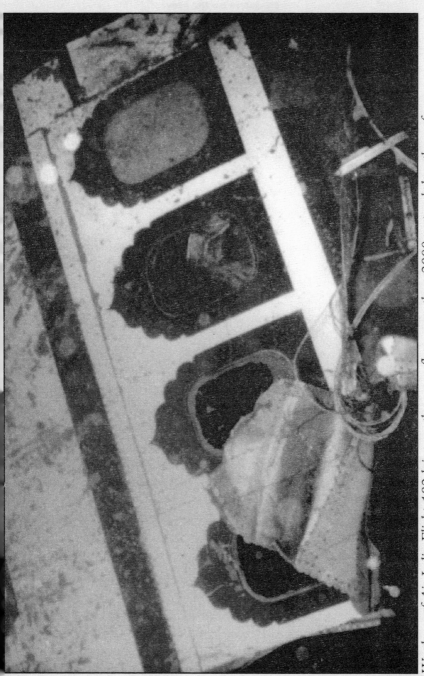

Wreckage of Air India Flight 182 lying on the ocean floor more than 2000 metres below the surface.
(Associated Press)

visiting family in India for the first time. Hoping that the disaster will never be repeated, airport officials set out to learn more about terrorists and their methods. They have become more strict and careful than ever, especially about checking suspicious baggage.

CHAPTER SEVEN

Recent Disasters

In recent years, Canadians have experienced some terrible disasters. Whether these events are floods, storms or aircraft crashes, they affect us all in some way. Some families mourn lost relatives, while others are involved in rescue or repair work. But whatever the nature of the trouble, and wherever in our country it occurs, disasters seem to bring Canadians together. It can be as simple as a message of sympathy or encouragement. It can be as complex as a community-wide food or clothing drive. It can be personal: using vacation time to travel to the scene and pitch in. It can be political: pushing government for better safety regulations, or signing petitions for victim compensation. Across our country, when bad things happen, people want to help.

The Crash of Swissair Flight 111

On September 2, 1998, in the cockpit of a wide-bodied jetliner, two Swissair pilots were involved in a heroic struggle. Just minutes before, smoke had begun to wisp from the ceiling into their cockpit. The pilots immediately put on oxygen masks and radioed for an emergency landing.

The smoke and heat got worse. Before long, they could barely see their instruments. In the ceiling above them, a fire burned hot enough to melt the aluminum and send it dripping down behind them. Suddenly all three electric power systems began to go out, causing most of the instruments to fail. Dense clouds and the black of night prevented the men from seeing anything out of their window. Captain Urs Zimmermann and co-pilot Stephan Loew could not even see lights on the ground to guide them and help them fly level.

In spite of these crises the men still managed to descend, dump extra fuel and make the correct turns toward Halifax airport, an airport neither of them had ever seen. Seconds passed. The large jet was over water, just minutes away from landing. Halifax air traffic control had been in steady radio contact with Swissair Flight 111, had given them permission to land, had cleared the skies of other aircraft to allow them in . . . but at 10:26 P.M. the pilots did not answer a final radio message.

Shortly after 10:30 P.M., people living around St. Margaret's Bay near Halifax heard a tremendous explosion out at sea. At the same time, phone calls from the Rescue Co-ordination Centre in Halifax were alerting ships and aircraft that a passenger jet was missing from radar. The search for a crash site and for survivors began. The HCMS *Preserver*, a naval supply ship, was nearby. Fishermen from many small communities along the coast joined in a rush to find and help survivors. Ambulances from every nearby village raced to the shoreline.

A few kilometres out on St. Margaret's Bay, the crash site was found. Reeking of jet fuel, a mixture of wreckage floated quietly on the water in the blackness of the night. The rescuers shone their lights on the water, hoping for survivors. They found only clothing, bits of wreckage, luggage, children's toys and human remains. For these people, the nightmare of what they saw could never be forgotten.

At the Queen Elizabeth II Hospital in Halifax, the Emergency department had been preparing for the worst possible situation. All available doctors, nurses and technicians had been called in. Patients were sent to other departments as the staff scrambled to get ready for the injured people to arrive — possibly up to 200 of them. For hours they waited. Finally a voice announced simply: "Thank you for coming. You can all go home." Dr. Doug Sinclair, head of the department, described it as a deeply sad moment. Clearly, not a single survivor was expected.

Swissair Flight 111 had been flying from New York to Geneva, Switzerland. It was a regular flight which was often taken by Americans and Swiss tourists, as well as members of the United Nations. On board was a Canadian UNICEF official, Yves de Roussan, American AIDS researcher Jonathan Mann, and Joseph LaMotta, son of the famous American boxer, "Raging Bull" Jake LaMotta. Included in the cargo of the doomed jet were millions of dollars' worth of cash, Swiss watches, diamonds and a painting by Picasso.

All 229 passengers and crew died instantly when Flight 111 crashed. Most of the cargo was completely destroyed. The MD-11 jet aircraft was smashed into millions of pieces, some no larger than a postage stamp. The complete devastation of the crash caused aviation experts to guess that the jet had crashed nose-first into the sea at over 600 kilometres per hour. At such speeds, hitting water is much the same as hitting concrete.

Investigators are still piecing together parts of the aircraft in an attempt to find the cause of the fire, but such work takes years. What is known is that electrical failure shut down essential instruments in the cockpit. Even the most experienced pilots in flight simulators will eventually "crash" if their instruments fail and they cannot see the horizon. The Swissair pilots had no chance. Unfortunately for the investigators, the loss of electrical power also caused the flight data recorder to fail. The last few minutes of Flight 111's history was not recorded.

Peggy's Cove, the town nearest to the crash site, is one of Canada's most beautiful. Its smooth-worn rocks, its lighthouse and the friendly wood-frame houses have been photographed by countless tourists over the years. The tragedy of September 2, 1998, brought hundreds of Swiss and American families to the tiny village. People in all the nearby communities opened their homes, or offered meals or transportation — or just a listening ear. As the Irish had done for the victims of the Air India Boeing 747 crash thirteen years before, the people of Nova Scotia reached out to those whose lives had been shattered.

The picturesque village of Peggy's Cove, N.S., is patrolled by police and rescue officials after a Swissair jet plunged into the ocean off the Nova Scotia coast, killing 229 people. (Canadian Press, Andrew Vaughan)

Storm of the Century

Millions of Canadians who live in eastern Ontario, Quebec and northern New Brunswick and Nova Scotia will long remember the Ice Storm of January, 1998. It broke all records as the costliest storm in Canada's history, taking twenty-five lives and causing more than a billion dollars' damage.

In early January unusual weather conditions brought on not just one, but two serious freezing rain storms. More than seventy millimetres of clear and heavy ice — double the amount of other bad storms — coated the Ottawa and St. Lawrence valleys, one of the most densely populated areas of Canada.

Although the ice-coated trees sparkled with picture-postcard beauty, they were dangerous: large branches weighing hundreds of kilograms snapped like toothpicks, tearing down hydro lines, destroying cars and damaging rooftops. A glaze of ice covered every street, making driving a nightmare. There was nothing people could do but watch it happen. Even the huge hydro towers that carry high-voltage power lines crumpled to the ground as if they were made of aluminum foil. Only one main major power line in Montreal remained intact, but barely, and it was in danger of failing at any time.

Over two million citizens in the Montreal area were left without power. Millions more shivered in the dark in Ottawa, Kingston, Brockville, Quebec, Trois Rivières and Saint John; and in rural areas as far east as the Annapolis Valley of Nova Scotia.

This was no ordinary power failure. It was not a matter of routing power from another direction or repairing a few hydro towers. There was so much damage, and it was so extensive, that Hydro Québec and Ontario Hydro began predicting it would take weeks to restore the power to some areas. Some of the country areas could expect to wait a month.

Montreal seemed quiet, almost deserted for many days. For more than a week at least 700 000 people there were without power. Most businesses were closed, even ones with power, for the danger of ice sheets falling from buildings discouraged people from making the trip downtown.

Schools and offices closed as their buildings cooled down and water pipes froze. People stayed at home, shivering under blankets and huddled near fires — if they were lucky enough to have a fireplace. Candles and oil lamps provided light in the evening and added a tiny bit of warmth. Many people cooked on camp stoves or barbecues. Others braved the treacherous streets to go to the nearest functioning restaurant. Long forgotten board games and decks of cards were brought out for entertainment, and families found a new closeness as they spent more than usual time together. Neighbours shared with each other, and people with power invited whole families of strangers to share their homes. Luckily the hospitals and nursing homes had their own emergency power generators, run by big diesel motors. For them it was business as usual.

Joshua and Denise Trimm, two young people from Dollard des Ormeaux, describe their experience, typical of many: "Our power went out for a full week. When it got too cold for us to stay at our house we went over to our grandma's house because there was still power in that part of Montreal. Two days after we got there, our grandma's power went out too.

"The next day we went across the street to a seniors' home to get some hot water. It had power and they invited us all in to keep warm. Everyone was kind and generous. They let us watch cartoons, made soup for us and let us play with their grandchildren's toys. People seemed to be friendlier during the ice storm.

"Every day our dad went to our house to check the power and clean up branches that had fallen. . . . There was so much ice on the branches that they were bent all the way down to the ground. When it got cold the tips of the branches froze right to the ground.

"Our dad brought home dry ice from his work and we used it to keep the fridge cold. . . . During the day we went to the shopping mall for something to do. At night the only lights you could see were the lights of the fire trucks and hydro workers or the blue and green flash of the transformers exploding. . . . It got dark very early so we used lots of candles. Grandma had a kerosene lantern but the smell made Joshua feel sick so we stopped using it. When the power came back on at our house our grandma

Hydro Québec high-voltage towers collapsed after the ice storm hit southwestern Quebec. The storm left more than a million households without electricity. (Canadian Press)

came to stay with us. Dad went back to our grandma's house to make sure the pipes weren't frozen and he found that someone had broken in to her house. They broke her back door down.

"My aunt Jill had a baby during the ice storm and when she had to leave the hospital, her power was still out. Her family came to stay with us too. There were always lots of people at our house. It was fun. We had no school for two weeks."

But soon the novelty of life without power began to wear thin. Day by day the cold continued to creep in from every direction. The lack of hot water for showers or baths made people miserable. Restaurants had huge lineups, for the people inside were reluctant to leave their warmth. High-rise apartment living became very unpleasant, as day after day, residents had to carry groceries and other necessities up countless gruelling flights of stairs.

It was more than unpleasant for others — it was overwhelming. Area hydro workers quickly fell behind in the herculean task of getting the power back on, and safely. Help came from all directions. Fleets of public utilities trucks and hydro workers came from the Atlantic provinces, Ontario and even Manitoba, and others from several American states came to help with the repair. Crews barely rested, working long hours for several weeks in extreme cold and icy conditions, stringing almost 3000 kilometres of new wire and setting more than 10 000 new poles in place. Thousands of electric generators were loaned from businesses and individuals from hundreds of kilometres around.

Farmers, especially those with dairy herds, needed electrical power to run their equipment. Farmers who had them shared portable generators, taking turns making power for several hours, then passing the generator on.

Canada's military responded in a big way. In the biggest peacetime gathering of Canadian troops ever, the soldiers joined forces with the hydro crews, police, firefighters and rescue workers to help in every way. Whether manning shelters, cutting up fallen trees or helping the hydro crews clean up wrecked towers, the military showed their ability to be organized, efficient and courageous.

Firefighters were challenged, as well. With so many home fireplaces put to twenty-four-hour use, fire was a constant danger. Ruby and Jeff Hoogsteen of Alfred, Ontario, know exactly how bad it could be. On a cold Wednesday evening they and their five young children were at a farm next door, helping a neighbour milk his cows.

"Jeff's watch was running slow, so we came home later than we had planned. . . . Jeff found that fire was spreading from a leak in our fireplace to the wood beams in the basement. If we had come home on time, we all would have been asleep on the top floor when it really started.

"I took the children out of the house while Jeff tried to put the fire out. He couldn't, so we grabbed a few photo albums and waited outside. The local fire department could not put it out either and so the whole house was burned to the ground.

"Still, the fire was a blessing. It was a test of our faith in God, because never before did we have to rely on Him to provide all our needs. Neighbours and complete strangers helped us in the weeks and months that passed. Members of our church 'walked their talk' and gave us everything we needed, a house to live in, toys, clothes, toothbrushes and toothpaste, and even 200 rolls of toilet paper."

Months after the storm ended, the ruin of the storm was still easy to see. Huge tree limbs continued to be cut and carted off for firewood well into the summer of 1998. There was lasting damage to many people's livelihoods, as well. Hectares of prized sugar maples were ruined for years to come. Manufacture of all kinds shut down, and businesses lost millions of dollars. Water damage from burst pipes added to the costs.

Still, those who sold gasoline-powered generators had a sales boom. The memory of weeks without electricity has made the people of the St. Lawrence and Ottawa valleys more cautious. They will not soon forget their "Storm of the Century."

Tragedy in Les Éboulements

There is a tiny beautiful island in Quebec called Île aux Coudres. It lies in the middle of the busy St. Lawrence River 100 kilometres east of Quebec City. To the north and south of it, rusty freighters from around the world push through the shipping lanes on their way to some of North America's greatest cities. Yet Île aux Coudres keeps its pleasant slow pace throughout the seasons and the years. The family names have not changed much since the time of Champlain. At one end of the island stands an old broken-down windmill. At the other end of the island is the Hotel La Roche Pleureuse, named for the "crying rock" nearby.

During the summer months hundreds of tourists come to see the old Quebec way of life and to stay a while in a place where crime and busy traffic are quickly forgotten. In the autumn, they come from all around to see the leaves in their brilliant oranges and reds. To get to the island, they take a car ferry. The ferry landing on the north shore of the St. Lawrence is in the town of Les Éboulements.

The road leading to Les Éboulements is one of the many curving, picturesque roads in the area, beautiful — and deadly. The final kilometre is all downhill, with a sharp turn at the bottom. Just that and a simple guardrail stand between vehicles and a twenty-metre fall into a ravine. In 1974, a bus making its routine drive down this hill became front page news. Its engine failed, and with it failed the power brakes and steering. The driver did what he could, then hung on in terror as the bus plunged into the ravine. Fifteen people died.

Area people discussed changing the roadway to remove the deadly curve, but the alternative would require the demolition of eleven houses, and put the only road in and out of the very popular Île aux Coudres out of commission for some time. Local residents asked that a better barrier be put up, at least. A few more warning signs were posted, but nothing more was done.

On Thanksgiving Day of 1997 another bus began its descent, slowly and carefully. It was an autumn colour tour for senior citizens from the nearby town of St. Bernard de Beauce, and the pleasant job of driving them belonged to Mercier Bus driver André Desruisseau. Then the job became a nightmare. The bus's brakes were badly worn, and halfway down the steep hill they failed completely. Desruisseau geared down and fought to control the bus's descent, but he could not. Gradually the stricken bus gained speed, whistling downward toward the deadly curve. The driver tried to slow the bus by running along the guardrail on his left. It did not work. Instead, the bus rammed through the guardrail and flew through the air. Seconds later it landed on its side in the bottom of the ravine.

Residents from all the houses nearby raced to the scene. Some had witnessed the whole terrible scene; one, André Castonguay, said it looked as if the bus had fallen into a hole. The rescuers were greeted by

Rescue workers surround a bus after it plunged into a ravine at the bottom of a hill in Les Éboulements. (Canadian Press QBCJ, Daniel Mallard)

a dreadful silence. "There was absolutely no reaction from inside the bus," said Father Jean Moisan, another of the first ones there. "I didn't hear anyone crying for help."

Fr. Moisan and the others helped shuttle the injured and the dead from the bus to a railroad bed nearby. From there, they were lifted to the roadway and brought to hospital.

Dr. Stephane Maurice assessed the forty-three dead, noting that they had died from head and chest injuries. The five survivors were seriously hurt, and one of them died shortly after. Nearly every family in St. Bernard de Beauce, a farming town of just over two thousand people, lost a relative or a friend in the accident. Half the members of the town's senior citizen's club were killed.

At the inquest, the bus's faulty brakes were blamed. Police confirmed that there were no skid marks found at the bottom of the hill. Still, Fr. Moisan was reminded of that other crash, twenty years earlier. It was terrible to see the same thing happen again. "It is horrible to realize nothing was done," he says.

On the peaceful island of Île aux Coudres, the leaves continued changing with autumn, and falling one by one. Forty-four people will never again see their beauty.

The Red River Flood

Knowing it was coming didn't make it much easier. In 1997 people in Manitoba knew they would have a "flood of the century." They knew it months before the water flowed through anyone's house, before anyone's farm was drowned in a sea of dirty brown water.

Weather forecasters know how a major flood will develop. They had seen all the signs pointing to this one. The previous year brought lots of rainfall, soaking deep into the soil until it could hold no more. Then came a long frosty winter, freezing the ground until it was like rock. All that was needed were heavy snowfalls and a late spring, so the snow would melt all at once and run off the surface into creeks and streams. Sure enough, the snows of 1997 came deeply, and residents began rebuilding the dikes around their homes. Then in early April a late winter blizzard dropped an incredible forty-three centimetres of snow. The big melt began in mid-April.

Just south of the Manitoba border, the town of Grand Forks, North Dakota, sits where the Red River begins to grow wide. The flood hit there first. On April 19, residents of Manitoba watched the TV news uneasily. They saw the flood overcome, one by one, the earthen dikes that the Americans had hastily piled up. The whole downtown area of Grand Forks was soon swamped with almost a metre of water. Electrical short-circuits caused fires above the

waterline; river and sewer water soaked into anything of value and made it trash.

The people of Winnipeg needed no more warning. They launched one of the biggest and most
costly projects in Canadian history.

Winnipeggers have had many floods before. The
area around Winnipeg is very flat, and water overflowing such a flat area spreads wide, like cola on a
countertop. In 1950 the Red River grew into a lake
of 1000 square kilometres and flooded 10 000 homes
in Winnipeg alone. The damage cost millions of dollars to repair. Since that flood, levees — or dikes, as
many call them — were raised around the Red
River's banks and a floodway, or side channel, was
built to divert flood water to the north. Many small
towns and homes outside Winnipeg already had permanent dikes built around them, a testament to
floods in the past.

Water engineers began to calculate how high the
1997 flood would go. One of the engineers, Ron
Richardson, discovered that one of the major dikes
was inadequate. To withstand the predicted peak
flood level, it would have to be made three metres
higher and twenty kilometres longer than it already
was. The peak flood levels would be there in three
days!

From all over the province, workers and
machines — 400 pieces of heavy equipment —
came to build. They didn't stop. At night, helicopters
continually dropped brilliant flares, to light the way
for the dike builders. Some of the truck drivers did

not even stop for a meal in eighteen hours. This vast undertaking was completed just in time. The waters began lapping at the base of the new dike as the last bulldozers packed down the last layer of dirt and plastic sheeting.

The water continued to rise, encircling towns and houses south of Winnipeg, which were protected by ring dikes. The police had orders to evacuate everybody, but many farmers and homeowners refused to leave. "This is my home and I am the only one who can protect it," said one man. These men and women stayed awake day and night, patrolling their dikes as the water crept higher, endlessly filling gaps with sandbags. In many heartbreaking cases the water won anyway, running over or bursting through the dikes and leaving a precious home soaked with polluted river water.

Sandbagging became a community affair. For kilometres around the Red River area everyone got involved. School children, office workers and senior citizens all turned out to fill sandbags. They filled, lifted, carried and placed sandbags until their arms were numb with the effort and their backs became too stiff to bend. New volunteers arrived by the hour and worked to exhaustion, protecting the houses of complete strangers.

Soldiers from all parts of Canada were also sent to the Winnipeg area to help. Armed Forces mechanic Steven Dusa was just one of many. He and his unit, the Royal Canadian Dragoons, travelled for three days from Petawawa, Ontario, where they were

A breach in the dike flooded the town of Ste. Agathe. (DND, Master Corporal Paul Howe)

based. They drove in armoured vehicles called Cougars, that are able to go on land and in water and would be useful in maintaining security in flooded areas. However, as with everyone else, their job turned into sandbagging. For three and a half weeks, they stayed to help. During those weeks Steven noticed the hospitality of the residents.

"In eleven years with the armed forces I have never seen such a friendly response from people. They brought racks of donuts from the local coffee shop. Someone else brought over a soft drink machine right in the parking lot where we were set up. People baked cookies and brought them out. Everywhere we went, people gave us things at half price because we were there to help them."

413 Squadron, Greenwood, Nova Scotia, checking out a possible evacuation just south of Ste. Agathe. (DND, Master Corporal Paul Howe)

By now the flood was forty kilometres wide just south of Winnipeg, and people were calling it "the Red Sea." But the dikes around Manitoba's capital city were holding. Aluminum boats and motorized rubber rafts became the essential vehicles. Carrying sandbags to isolated houses, bringing groceries or bottled water, or ferrying people to their property was a job only for boats. Sometimes their propellers clipped submerged road signs or treetops in the vast and churning sea.

Roads, fields and railway tracks had disappeared beneath the brown waves of silty water. Houses and barns stood here and there, telling tales of financial ruin. Beneath the floods, well water was now mixed with sewage, and grain bins and silos were useless masses of sodden waste. Five hundred homes in the town of Ste. Agathe . . . One hundred and fifty homes in Grand Point . . . These areas had not flooded in a hundred years, until now.

Informed by hourly radio and TV news broadcasts, people all over Canada started counting up the centimetres and counting down the hours. Engineers had predicted when the peak flood levels would come. Would the new, huge dikes hold? As they waited, ordinary Canadians far away from the Red River area searched their attics and basements for spare clothing, food and clean-up rags, to send them to those at the front line of the destruction.

There was a noisy celebration once the peak flood levels had passed and the waters began to recede. The dikes had held! Then the clean-up began, and the clean-up was to last much longer than the flood. Once again, total strangers came to the rescue. People arrived from all parts of Canada, ready to help.

A youth group in a small Ontario church decided to go, and their leaders, Pat and Dan Koets, helped them organize. First they raised funds: about $5000, for gas and expenses. Along the way, hotels and restaurants gave discounts when they learned the kids were going to help with the flood. Once there, they joined a clean-up crew organized by the Mennonite church. The crew provided food and a place to stay, and sent the volunteers out on jobs. Pat describes the work they did:

"Dan would use a power washer to wash the basements with Javex and water and the kids and I would scrub and sweep the water into the drains. You would see these beautiful homes belonging to seniors. They had put everything into them for their retirement and now they were such a mess. Outside you would see a portable toilet and all their drinking water would have to be brought in bottles.

"On our last day we went to a farm to help remove hay bales that had been soaked. It took four of us to lift each one. The farmer had stayed during the flood to patrol the dike around his property. The dike was breached on the very last day of the flood. It was such a heartbreak for him."

The Koets's son, Chris, was part of another crew. "We were helping an old man in a small house and he had lost everything. He couldn't even afford food so he was given meals by the Mennonites the same as we were. We would be removing stuff that was totally wrecked and he would look it over still, to see if it could be used in some way. The man cried. He had nothing left. Just before we left my friend Mike and I drove out to his place and gave him the rest of the money we had saved."

Singer/actor Tom Jackson organized the Red River Relief Concert to help the victims of the flood. He contacted just about every musician in Manitoba, and almost all of them came through. On May 8, 50 000 people watched their favourite musicians perform. Former rock stars Burton Cummings and Randy Bachman appeared together on stage for the first time in years, reviving tunes from their glory days.

Insurance companies and the government promised to help pay for the losses as well. But so much of what was lost was irreplaceable. The only gain was the knowledge that strangers could become good friends in times of need.

The Saguenay Flood

The summer of 1996 was supposed to be a good one for the Saguenay region of Quebec — the province's heartland. Its high rate of unemployment was offset by tourism: many Canadians and foreign tourists liked to come to the region, whale-watching on the Saguenay River, boating and camping on Lac St.-Jean and attending festivals and celebrations. Hotels and restaurants counted on the summer season to help them pay bills and stay in business for the rest of the year. The town of Laterrière was celebrating its 150th anniversary and many festivities were planned for that happy event.

But as can often happen, the weather interfered with everyone's plans. Heavy rainfall hit the area for weeks in late spring and early summer, and the many dams in the area were already full. The rains began again on Friday, July 19, and they continued almost non-stop for forty-eight hours until they had dropped over twenty centimetres. This was as much rain in two days as the region would normally get in a month, and it broke all records.

The situation got worse.

The owners of some dams wisely let the water flow out to prevent them from overflowing and sending a sudden torrent of water downstream. But problems began at the Kenogami reservoir. Cranes used for lifting dam gates on two of the dams failed, and not enough water was released. The added rainfall caused the water of Kenogami Lake to build up to impossible levels. When the Kenogami dams finally began to overflow, millions of litres of lake water were sent rushing downstream toward Chicoutimi. Like a tidal wave, the water swept houses off the banks and into the water as if they had been made of paper. Other dams in the region overflowed or burst with the added burden of water. The flood was unstoppable.

Radio stations warned people by the hour and most were able to pack a few cherished possessions and leave before the relentless flood waters hit. But some roads in nearby Jonquière and La Baie and along the Saguenay River were washed away as easily as sandcastles at a beach. There was nothing for many to do but stay on high ground and watch as small creeks became raging rivers, tearing away at everything in their path. Hundreds of people saw their homes destroyed, all their possessions washed away and their cars carried along like chips of wood in a creek.

Some lost even more. In La Baie, the swollen waters of the Ha! Ha! River triggered a mud slide which demolished the Paquet-Garceau home. Though the parents and one child escaped with their lives, young Mathieu and Andrea, aged nine and seven, were killed by the mud, despite the frantic efforts of twenty rescuers to get at them. People who attempted to drive across washed-out roads found their cars had become death traps, holding the occupants inside as they rolled and bounced downstream with the flood, filling with muddy water. All

A downtown Chicoutimi street is cut off by rising waters. Floods in the region forced over 10 000 residents to be evacuated. (Jacques Boissinot)

told, seven people died and $700 million worth of damage was done.

The Canadian military came out in full force, working with heroic energy through the crisis. Helicopters buzzed continually overhead, picking people up from homes and areas of high ground. Canadian Forces Base Bagotville became a temporary home to thousands of evacuated residents.

The floods also brought sympathy from the rest of Canada. Banks and organizations across the nation accepted donations for the flood victims. The Red Cross set a goal to raise two million dollars. Very soon an amazing twenty-two million dollars had come in. Although a few people pointed out that the Saguenay was the heart of the Quebec separatist movement, most Canadians asked no questions, but simply sent money and help.

Said Reginald Gervais, a city councillor in Jonquière, who had voted "yes" to separation months before: "You cannot help but feel more Canadian and appreciate being Canadian." He asked reporters, "Can you say thank you for us?"

Westray Mine Disaster

"The most important thing to take out of a mine is the miner."
> — *LePlay, French Inspector General of Mines, 1872.*

Trevor Jahn and Ferris Dewan were quiet as they rode underground at the start of a long twelve-hour shift in the Westray coal mine. They had been friends since elementary school, and had worked in various mines together from one end of the country to the other. They were good miners and had always enjoyed their work.

Yet both men were nervous. Miners are not normally nervous people — they cannot afford to be. But this new and supposedly modern mine was the most dangerous place they had ever worked in. Rock falls were so common that the men had stopped counting the number of times they had jumped out of the way to avoid being hit by falling slabs of coal. All coal mines produce poisonous and explosive methane gas, but proper fresh air ventilation systems continually remove it and keep the gas well below danger levels. At Westray, however, the ventilation system was not working properly, and the methane was found to be at high levels. Coal dust also was being allowed to build up in work areas, and it can explode violently and burn quickly.

Both Trevor Jahn and Ferris Dewan knew how a coal mine should be operated. Coal mines can be made reasonably safe, but Westray wasn't. Even aside from the amount of explosive and flammable material around, the men were being given equipment to use which could give off sparks — equipment that was strictly against the law for use in coal mines.

Jobs were scarce and many men might have been happy to have steady work, but Jahn had had enough. He was saving his money in order to leave this mine. On May 8, 1992, he was about two weeks short of his goal.

Miles Gillis, another miner with many years' experience, also came to work daily fearing for his life. He was so certain that an explosion would occur, he had shown a friend a map of the Westray mine and pointed out the southwest section, saying that was where the blast would happen. He also predicted that all the men working in that area would be killed. Though he tried to hide his fears from his wife at first, in time he told her how afraid he was. With tears in his eyes, he made his wife promise to call for an investigation into the mine's practices if the blast should happen while he was underground.

Westray miners had reported the unsafe conditions to the mine managers and the government, but nothing much was done. Many of the men had signed a contract in which they promised to stay at Westray for a year. They felt they couldn't leave. The mine was the only steady work many of them had had in years.

In the early morning hours of May 9, a spark from one of the mining machines ignited the high-level methane gas in the southwest section, just as

Miles had predicted. The sudden flash sent a fatal shock wave and a wall of flame ripping through the mine. All twenty-six men in the mine that night were killed. After the flame had died down, the wreckage-filled tunnels were silent and dark. Trevor Jahn and Ferris Dewan, friends in life, were together also in death.

Shaun Comish was one of the lucky ones. He, too, had wondered if he would be killed by a rock-fall or an explosion in this mine. He had come off the day shift just hours before the blast, and came back the day after — this time as a draegerman, to look for possible survivors. He described it this way:

"I could not believe my eyes as we walked down into what can only be called hell. There was a smell I can't really describe, a smell of burning, mixed with the smell of pulverized rock. There was a hard black coating on the down-ramp side of all the pipes and arches. The mine had a deafening silence — no fans, no humming transformers, just nothing, nothing at all. All the walls were covered with a black coating of burnt dust and debris. It was like the inside of a cannon barrel that had been loaded with anything and everything. The further down we went, the worse it looked. Cement bulkheads that had been [up to a metre] thick had been smashed into little pieces and thrown [thirty metres] or more. Steel doors that had been [five metres] high and [four metres] wide were now crumpled, twisted pieces of strange-looking metal. Two transformers had been smashed together so hard they looked like one hunk of debris. These transformers, which weigh roughly seven tonnes each, had been thrown about [thirty metres] across the [tunnel] and down the decline.

"In the Number Nine [tunnel] all the arches were knocked over like dominoes, and the conveyor belt was underneath them. Sheets of metal and [large] timbers were thrown all around . . . It made our walking slow and extremely dangerous. There was the fear that the methane gas in this area was in the explosive range. One spark from any metal-on-metal contact might set it off.

"I looked up the drift ahead of a wrecked boom truck and I could see some of the bodies of the second group of men lying there. I lowered my eyes and asked God to be kind to their souls and to give their family comfort and strength to get through this horrible ordeal. I recall seeing one man lying there. His face was covered, but I knew who he was and I felt a lump form in my throat. It hurt me very much to see these men taken from us, all for the sake of greed. I took a deep breath and told myself to put it out of my mind for now and get these guys out to their families. We placed our man onto the stretcher and the team headed back out of this manmade hell."

The next day Shaun Comish returned with other draegermen. By now, few people believed they would find any of the men alive.

"Ahead we saw a fall of rock that went higher than the roof. It was impossible to go on. Just as we turned to go back we heard the rumble of another rock fall. Tons of rock were falling somewhere in the

An aerial view of the entrance to the Westray mine after the explosion. (Canadian Press, Kerry Doubleday)

darkness. This scared us completely. Just as we rounded a corner in the tunnel we heard another rock fall and we felt a change of air pressure. We all thought the same thing. Were we trapped in? We discussed it and decided to go on. A few minutes later we felt another change in pressure in our ears. That meant a big rock fall somewhere else. We talked about it again and decided to get out. The way back to surface was as difficult as coming down, but there were no more rock falls as we were leaving. Luckily as we climbed up piles of rocks we found our way had not been blocked.

"I left the mine site feeling I had let the families of the miners down. If we had gotten even one more man out it would have made a big difference in the way I was feeling. But it was not to be."

Only fifteen bodies of the twenty-six men in the mine were recovered. Shaun Comish never returned to mining. Now he works as a computer consultant.

The families of the dead men and the off-duty miners who had escaped death demanded a proper inquiry. It became the most important cause in their lives to see that their brothers, sons and fathers not be buried and forgotten with the mine. The fear that another Westray could happen again has driven them on.

They are also trying to bring criminal charges against some of the mine managers. Mine managers were pointedly blamed in Justice K. Peter Richard's report on the detailed investigation of the Westray mine disaster. Justice Richard also partially blamed the Government of Nova Scotia's Departments of Natural Resources and Labour, for not enforcing the rules. So many violations of safe mining practice were uncovered during the investigation that Justice Richard titled his report: "The Westray Story, A Predictable Path to Disaster."

May the shame of this disaster prevent another like it.

PHOTO CREDITS

ABOUT THE AUTHOR

René Schmidt has been a miner, construction worker, truck driver and taxi driver. He also worked
briefly on a Great Lakes freighter. Currently he is a
teacher with the Kawartha Pine Ridge School
Board. René lives with his family near Brighton,
Ontario.